Julian Clary is a comedian, enterta~~iner~~ ~~who has~~ toured the world with his one-man s~~hows. He began working~~ on the cabaret circuit in the early 1980s as 'The Joan Collins Fan Club' and then went on to appear in numerous TV shows as well as starring in a number of West End productions and the London Palladium pantos. As an author, Julian has published several books, including his *Sunday Times* bestselling memoir *A Young Man's Passage,* three novels and his children's series *The Bolds.* Julian has recently been presented with the LGBT Out and Proud award and the 2018 *Attitude* award for comedy. He lives in London with his husband and their two dogs, Albert and Gigi.

'Those of us of a certain age remember Fanny the Wonder Dog, but the caustic comic brings his other canine companions vividly to life too'
                                                                                                    Daily Telegraph

'Clary does write so beautifully about his dogs. He describes Albert as "compact and muscular, with short legs that turn outwards like the balletic supports of a Queen Anne footstool"'
                                                                                                    The Times

'I loved *The Lick of Love.* It's often insightful, sometimes hilarious, frequently filthy – I'm a cat person, but if anything were ever to convince me to get a dog, it would be this'
                                                                    Joanne Harris. Author of *Chocolat*

'I felt the Licks of Love on every page . . . It's quite simply an uplifting read, with bits of drama and tears thrown in'
                                                                                                    Dana Gillespie

Julian
Clary

The Lick of Love

How dogs changed my life

QUERCUS

First published in hardback in Great Britain in 2021 by
Quercus Editions Ltd

QUERCUS

This paperback edition published in 2022 by

Quercus Editions Ltd
Carmelite House
50 Victoria Embankment
London EC4Y 0DZ

An Hachette UK company

Copyright © 2021 Julian Clary

The moral right of Julian Clary to be
identified as the author of this work has been
asserted in accordance with the
Copyright, Designs and Patents Act, 1988.

All rights reserved. No part of this publication
may be reproduced or transmitted in any form
or by any means, electronic or mechanical,
including photocopy, recording, or any
information storage and retrieval system,
without permission in writing from the publisher.

A CIP catalogue record for this book is available
from the British Library

PB ISBN 9781 52941 253 6
Ebook ISBN 978 1 52941 251 2

Quercus Editions Ltd hereby exclude all liability to the extent
permitted by law for any errors or omissions in this book and for any loss,
damage or expense (whether direct or indirect) suffered by a
third party relying on any information contained in this book.

10 9 8 7 6 5 4 3 2

Typeset by CC Book Production
Printed and bound in Great Britain by Clays Ltd, Elcograf S.p.A.

Papers used by Quercus Editions Ltd. are from well-managed forests
and other responsible sources.

For Fanny, Valerie, Albert and Gigi

Contents

PART FOUR

Gigi

'The life that was lived was the best that could be done.'[1]

Fay Weldon *Auto da Fay*

Introduction

I have always followed my urges. Without question. The need to do, say, possess or swallow something sweeps through me like a primal scream and opposition is pointless. An urge is, after all, defined as a 'strong, restless desire', and we meddle with nature at our peril.

So when the mantra 'Get a dog!' started whirring in my youthful mind, I had to comply. It wasn't sensible, of course. I was twenty-one, living in one room in Blackheath, south-east London, with no particular idea of what direction my life would take. I had vague thoughts of being a performer and had enjoyed premonitions of fame and celebrity since the age of thirteen, but these were mere daydreams and I can't claim any real sense of destiny. I had recently applied for a job with Help the Aged because I liked the company of old people and had a taste for Murray Mints.

But I followed my urges and got a dog . . . and within a few years she had propelled me up the ranks of the alternative comedy circuit and onto television.

There is a lot of stern advice available to anyone wondering if they should get a dog: Are you ready? Can you give a dog a happy life? Can you afford it? Do you have time? Then, apparently, you have to choose what sort of dog you'd like, what size, gender, age, and so on. I didn't do any of this. I acted on impulse. I followed a need as compelling as the need to eat or drink.

The 'Get a dog!' compulsion was to return again nineteen years later on 5 November, when I was in a shopping centre in Sutton, of all places, filming a Daz advert. It was stronger this time, and more urgent.

'I need a puppy!' I cried to my assistant Bertha. Fame, the reader may observe, had made me a tad petulant. This sudden need for a dog was to occur again on two more occasions, each time a bit more extreme, like a career criminal taking greater risks as his crimes escalate in an attempt to recreate the first, thrilling rush. In 2009 I was in the middle of a chat show when the host brought on a selection of homeless puppies. I had taken a liking to one within seconds, and took him home. Then in 2019 I locked eyes with a photograph of a dog in a Serbian rescue pound and I sent for her. What next? Will I be snatching dogs from the arms of their owners on the street?

So my need for a dog (or two) in my life is not to be resisted, that much is clear. Dogs bring calmness and clarity to my life. There is much talk these days about the benefits of mindfulness and living in the moment, but you don't need to become a Buddhist or go to the trouble of reading a book by Ruby Wax if you have a dog to interact with. One stroke is all it takes, as the rent boy said to the bishop.

Throughout my adult life there has been a dog by my side, bearing witness, radiating unconditional love or just snoring peacefully. Whatever else is going on, it is the water bowl in the kitchen, the dog hair on my jumper, the knowing gaze from the dog in the basket beside me that comforts me and tells me that all is well. I am not the first person to observe that dogs are uplifting for the human spirit.

I have a theory: what if each dog has been 'sent' to us to help us learn something profound, to enrich our lives and help us evolve spiritually, like cards dealt to us by an all-seeing deity? It's a thought-provoking wheeze, if nothing else, but stop me if I'm coming over all Dalai Lama. We can blame the herbal tea.

It is only now that I can fully appreciate the contribution of my four-legged friends. They deserve this book. Without them, my life might have veered off towards a number of undesirable destinations. I feel the need to articulate my appreciation and thanks.

My first dog, Fanny, came into my life when I was twenty-one and somewhat adrift. At the time I was an aspiring performer, unsure which porthole to stick my head through. Her zest for life and willingness to try every new experience helped me to become bolder than I think I would otherwise have been. More importantly, as I took my first tentative steps on the comedy circuit, she provided the star quality that would otherwise have been sadly lacking.

Fanny was also my guardian angel. I like to think she still is. (You will get used to my tendency to etherealise.) She stopped bad things from happening to me, just as a St Christopher medal protects the traveller. I hate to break this to you but I was, in my youth, a rather unfussy picker-up of gentlemen callers, oblivious to the risks involved – or maybe just willing to take my chances. Fanny saw off several men who had evil intent, sometimes simply by her presence. St Sebastian is considered the patron saint of homosexuals but I think Fanny the Wonder Dog might be his understudy, should he be feeling under the weather due to all those pesky arrows in his ivory flesh.

Valerie, my whippet crossbreed, escorted me through my forties, urging kindness where otherwise petulance might have triumphed. Poised and fearless, the Germaine Greer to my Bernard Manning, she kept things in proportion, as if to say: 'Showbiz is not all of life. I am here. I care nothing for your profile, bank account, TV series or magazine covers. Now pick up my shit and shut the fuck up.'

Ten years later, she was joined by Albert, a jaunty geezer type, sent to acclimatise me to middle age, perhaps, to instruct me about the benefits of peace, quiet and an afternoon nap, and to help me seduce my future husband, mediate between us and prevent him from slipping through my fingers.

Most recently there has been Gigi: a fur bullet, an inscrutable, unpredictable, hilarious acid trip of a dog. Gigi has expanded the boundaries of love beyond where I thought they lay, and proved that there are no limits.

Without these four dogs – well, there would be nothing to write about.

PART ONE
Fanny

'Dogs never bite me. Just humans.'

– Marilyn Monroe

CHAPTER 1

Urges in South-East London

There were three tenants in three rooms in the Blackheath flat I lived in, and there was a payphone in the hallway, from which I dialled South London Dog Rescue. It wasn't a dog rescue charity in the conventional sense – it had no kennels staffed by outdoorsy types in monogrammed polo shirts. It was just a kind, animal-loving woman on the end of the phone.

'We've been told about a dog in distress in a pet shop,' she said in answer to my enquiry about dogs in need of a home. 'It's in a very cramped cage, not well looked after, and it's been there for weeks.'

I wrote down the address and said I'd go and see the dog the next day. This meant I had the night to think about what I was doing. Really, it wasn't a good idea. I was twenty-one and footloose. I called my mother, who said all the appropriate things: a dog is a tie, you're not settled, you have no job. No doubt she was worried that she and my father would end up looking after it once the novelty had worn off.

'So I suppose you'd better go and get it,' she finally said. She sounded a little cross and exasperated but also, I decided, encouraging. My mother was a big fan of spontaneous acts. She had to say the right, sensible things, but I told myself there was a subtext to what she was saying. Be reckless.

'If you think about it for too long, you'd never do anything' was one of her sayings. When she and my father got married and had my sister, they had no carpets on the floor – but they bought a top-of-the-range London Baby Coach pram.

Our family's first experience of owning a dog when I was a child had come about by another of my mother's impulsive acts. Each summer we would pile into my father's Ford Zephyr and set off for Cornwall for two weeks. We stayed in a little cottage near St Ives. I have memories of us on the beach, sheltering behind a canvas windbreak, investigating rock pools and other traditional activities. As is the way with British holidays, the weather was unreliable. One year, when I was aged about seven, it rained relentlessly for the entire fortnight. My mother has a gift for telling long, improvised stories that could, if necessary, go on for days. When we were stuck inside our cottage during those long, wet August days, one of the stories she made up was truly epic. It involved a family, much like ours, who were on holiday in Cornwall when it rained and rained and never stopped. I think floods were involved, and they might have bobbed out to sea for a while in a tin bath, but they made it home in time for a cream tea. As she was making it up as she went along, the story would be inspired by whatever happened to be around. We'd go on long country drives in the rain. If we passed a man with a beard, then it was a fair bet that the story would suddenly feature just such a character. In his beard would live a mouse who would come out at night and nibble on the Cornish pasty crumbs that were stuck there. If we passed a windmill, then that would be where the man lived.

One day, my mother told us that the fictional family piled into their car and went on a drive. Down a country lane they saw a sign that read 'Puppies for Sale'. They went in through the gate and there was a litter of puppies. The family chose an adorable puppy and took it home with them. Their holiday was saved – transformed from disaster to triumph, just like that.

'And that's what we're going to do tomorrow!' concluded my mother.

'Really?' asked my father, choking on his coffee. It was the first he'd heard about it. But we children were squealing with excitement, of course, so it was too late for discussion. So that's how, the next day, we acquired a miniature long-haired dachshund puppy that we named Monty. In hindsight, it was not an outstanding success – no reflection on the dog. He was delightful for a while and I remember how thrilled my sisters and I were, and how we fought over him, jealously demanding possession. I don't think we had much idea of how to treat or train a puppy. He grew, as puppies do. But then he grew some more, until it was clear there was nothing 'miniature' in his genes whatsoever.

I thought it was a good game to get down on the floor and pretend to be a dog too, playing tug-of-war and growling and yapping. This went wrong one day when he was being fed and I tried to take his food away. Monty bit me. It was my fault, and my parents pointed this out. But as the months passed, he started to snap quite often. He bit my sister and my mother too. He was quite a cross dog. My father understood him best and always excused Monty's bad-tempered ways – until he bit my father. Then my father decided that the dog had to go. We were all very upset, so to soften the blow my parents told us that Monty would be going to live with my grandparents in Norfolk, so we would still see him during the school holidays. So off he went. He continued to grow in every direction until he was Cyril Smith with fur. A quiet life in the country suited him better. He lived to a ripe old age and never caused any trouble again.

Monty was the only dog we had when I was growing up. The 1970s was a rather frantic decade: both my parents were working and I had a long journey to school and back. We went for cats instead. We had two, Cindy and Robinson, but I wanted one of my own. Being told that Robinson could be 'mine' if I liked wasn't good enough. So aged eleven, I brought a kitten home from a pet shop in Richmond, despite being told very firmly that I wasn't allowed another cat.

'You'll take that straight back!' thundered my father.

My mother had been observing the scene. As I left the house, sobbing, the black and white kitten tucked inside my school blazer, she put her hand on my arm and said, 'If they won't take him back, then we'll have to keep him, I suppose. . .'.

And we did.

Now, as a young adult, I found myself in the grip of a new impulse – and this time it was the puppy in distress that was occupying my thoughts. After calling the lady from the South London Dog Rescue, I lay awake all that night thinking. Things always seem negative in the dark, I find, and worry and anguish flooded through me. How could I look after a dog? What if my landlady objected? Supposing I didn't like it? What would happen when I found a job?

And what about my nocturnal activities? I had been more or less unemployed for the last two years, since I'd left university. To say I had dipped my toe into the gay scene would be an understatement. I had immersed myself as if it were a jacuzzi. I was popular. By which I mean, available. Well, why not? I went out most nights with my friend Steven, a handsome, funny Irishman from Belfast with a gift for living in the moment that made him exciting company. Steven could lock eyes with a man on a train or the street and, through willpower and charisma, lead him astray on the spot. We would stroll to the bars and clubs of Soho and Earl's Court and we very rarely went home alone. I would end up in all sorts of dodgy places, waking up entwined with a man whose name escaped me. How could I leave the dog all night? Well, I could either change my sluttish ways or drag my booty back to Blackheath with me. And there was always Cathy, a nurse who lived in the room next to me. She would dog-sit. As would Nick, my best (and only) friend from school, who lived nearby.

There was another factor in all this. I was prone to being infatuated by unattainable men. I got sex and love confused quite often and would be left hankering after random men I had spent a few torrid hours with. Then I would drag Steven with me to the bar I had met Henry or Jacques or whoever in, hoping for a reunion that never happened. Consequently, I was often heartbroken and bereft. Then the only solution was to find someone new, which of course I did. I think, perhaps unconsciously, I thought a dog would take care of these unfulfilled, unreciprocated needs.

But most of my anguish that night was about the dog. I didn't know what it looked like or even what gender it was, but I kept seeing the pitiful creature, fear in its eyes, staring through a wire mesh cage, whimpering, waiting to be rescued. Having heard about the dog's plight, I couldn't leave it now. It was as if I had already passed that cramped cage and was being drawn back to it. The gift of liberty, of kindness, was mine to give.

I got up early the next morning and walked from my flat in Hardy Road to Lewisham High Street to catch the bus to the location. Rescuing that dog from its current circumstances suddenly felt urgent. I couldn't bear the animal to suffer for a moment longer than was necessary. I was trembling, I realised. Scared, as if I was about to do something reckless, which in a way I was. But it's something good, I reasoned with myself. I'm not going shoplifting.

I remember the cramped, chaotic pet shop and the gruff, unshaven old man who ran it. I don't think he liked gays (and I was very gay, in my sleeveless T-shirt and ripped jeans and with my tousled blond hair). I looked around, but there was no sign of a dog anywhere.

'I've heard about a dog that needs a home,' I said.

The old man grunted and jerked his head towards the back of the shop. I followed him out into a dark, shadowy yard piled with wood, cardboard boxes, rusted corrugated iron panels and assorted rubbish.

'She's in there,' he said, pointing to a rotten rabbit hutch. 'Can't shift her. No one wants her.'

I squatted down to peer inside. The hutch didn't look big enough to contain a dog, unless she was very tiny indeed. Then I saw a pair of round, dark eyes shining. Hopeful, confused, but not scared.

'Hello,' I said quietly. She came forward immediately and pressed her head to the roof of the hutch and her cheek to the wire. Her back feet scratched the wet sawdust in her attempt to push herself forward more, and her front paws came up to the wire on either side of her face as if she might squeeze through to me. I put my hand to the wire. Her tongue darted out and curled around my finger, back and out again. From the back of her throat a high-pitched whine communicated a desperate need for help.

'How long has she been in here?' I asked the man, trying not to sound too aghast.

'Few months. Can't shift her.'

'Can I get her out?' I asked.

He shrugged and gave a short-tempered huff. 'Yup.'

The door of the rabbit hutch was secured with some bent nails. I fiddled unsuccessfully with them, and the inhabitant began to whimper.

'Here,' said the man crossly and pushed me aside. He turned the nails, opened the door, lifted the wriggling puppy out by the scruff of her neck and put her in my arms. She immediately pushed her head under my chin. I held her pitifully thin chest with one hand and her trembling legs with the other, and could feel her heart pounding.

'Oh dear, dear,' I said. I tried to pull my head back to have a look at her, but she was glued to my neck. She smelled musty. Of sawdust, fear and urine.

'I know,' I said. 'Poor little sausage.'

My billing and cooing was a bit much for the shop owner, who exhaled loudly and rubbed his eyes. 'I'll be in the shop,' he said and left me alone in the yard with the dog. I didn't stop there long. Nowadays, if you rescue a dog there is paperwork, adoption fees and microchipping to take care of, but not in 1980. The shop owner wanted a fiver for the dog, so I obliged. I carried her out straight away, having barely looked at her, and didn't let go of her until I got back to my flat. I put her down in the kitchen. After several months in a rabbit hutch, it took her a few moments to move from a crouching position. She more or less froze, as if unable to cope with the change in her circumstances. Eventually she stretched her neck and looked around, wide-eyed. While she took it all in, I was able to see for the first time the dog that was now mine.

She was petite but elegant. Light and feline, like a whippet. She had short hair and her back and long, gently curving tail were black, fading to a warm honey colour across her shoulders and down her legs, with a white belly and matching paw tips. Her face was the same honey colour, but her extremities slowly grew to black again. Her eyes, which I would spend so much time gazing into, were brandy coloured with sparkling black pupils. They were enhanced with dark upward-sweeping markings on the outer sides, like an ancient Egyptian pharaoh. Most strikingly, she was beautifully symmetrical, both in markings and posture.

She was the loveliest creature I had ever seen. A sudden sob pulsated in my throat. I thought my heart would burst with love.

I got her a bowl of water and she drank most of it then sat down, tidying any drops of water on her chin or whiskers with her tongue. Now she looked at me with a mixture of amusement and inquisitiveness.

I sat on the floor next to her and she leant forward, sniffing me several times before licking the back of my hand. She licked for so long that I eventually moved my hand and stroked her head, which caused her to raise her head, freeze and close her eyes. Slowly her ears relaxed and I leant forward to kiss her gently on the nose, then she licked the side of my face. The pair of us sat there on the kitchen floor for some time, getting to know each other. After more stroking and licking, I patted my lap but she looked away shyly. She sat stiffly, looking questioningly at me, not sure of what was expected of her. After stroking her head again, I slid my hand down her shoulder and under her front leg, then slowly lifted her paw and held it, gently massaging the pad before placing it on my leg. She dropped her head a little and her body softened. It took me a while, but slowly I eased her onto my lap. She sat there awkwardly, as if expecting to be thrown off, before suddenly flopping down with a noisy sigh. Her limbs relaxed, her eyes closed and she curled into a ball, her tail wrapped around her face and over her ear with a slow, balletic flourish, as if she were silently rehearsing the entrance of the shades in *La Bayadère*. While she slept, I traced small circular movements across her head and ears, enjoying the sound of her breathing.

I had much to think about. She was here now. I was responsible for her. Life would never be the same.

CHAPTER 2

Laser Love

I'm not sure how long I had been asleep for, sitting on the kitchen floor, leaning against the wall. I woke up when Cathy, my flatmate, came home. She was a nurse at Greenwich Hospital, where she worked on the geriatric ward. She had porcelain skin, cupid lips painted frosty pink and a halo of white-blonde candyfloss hair.

'Let's have a look at her, then,' she said, taking off her coat and lighting a cigarette. The dog wagged her tail and moved in for a tentative lick. Once up and awake, she seemed to need to burn off some energy, I guess, after her long weeks of confinement. Cathy and I stood open-mouthed as she created a circular route around the kitchen: onto a bean bag, two chairs, the table, the kitchen counter and, with an athletic leap, back onto the floor again. This was repeated with increased speed until we were giddy watching. Giggles turned to wide-eyed horror when drops of liquid splashed on our faces as she passed. She was sprinting and having a wee at the same time. Remarkable, really. Some sort of canine celebration of her new-found liberty, perhaps. When she did slow down – between us, we managed to block her route – I held her in my arms. We got J Cloths and the mop out, and spent some time cleaning up. There was urine up the walls, over the windows and dripping from the light fitting.

'Such a clever dog,' observed Cathy. 'I'd better take my uniform off and put it in the wash. My old dears might not like dog's piss. Mind you, they don't seem to have any objection to their own.'

I carried the dog down to the patch of ground behind the flats, where she made herself comfortable. Back in my room I laid her on my bed and stroked her, wondering what name would suit her. I wanted something proper, something that would imply a dog of some substance. Margaret and Maureen were strong contenders for a few hours, until the word 'Fanny' just came out of my mouth spontaneously. Who knows what thought process preceded it? I knew it was right because she pricked up her ears and looked at me knowingly. So that was it.

Fanny settled in very quickly. I got a cardboard box from the corner shop and made her a bed with cushions and old towels, which I placed next to my bed that evening, so I could give her a reassuring stroke in the night. But one thing led to another and she got on the bed, then in it within ten minutes. I slept on my side, spooning her, her head resting on my arm, covers pulled up over her shoulder. She didn't snore but made contented sighs, and if I stroked her ribcage, she emitted a pleasant, tuneless wheezing sound, like a novelty bagpipe.

I took her to a vet the next day for her injections, worming tablets and flea treatment. Fanny was undernourished, he said, but otherwise fit and healthy. She was a lurcher, which just means a cross between a sighthound and a terrier – characterised by doggy types as gentle, loving, affectionate and loyal.

'She could be anything,' the vet said. 'There's probably a bit of whippet in there.' Fanny was about four months old.

It soon became apparent that Fanny's main interest was food. She hadn't had much of it, and never recovered from the hunger she must have felt in her early months. She always consumed her own food as a matter of urgency, but I was never able to teach her any manners or restraint regarding my own, or anyone else's. She'd eat anything in a flash. Off the table, out of the bin, in the street, from a passing child's hand. Even if it wasn't food. I learned my lesson early on when I left my dinner on the table to answer the phone in the hallway. It was lamb chops with potatoes and vegetables. I was only gone a few seconds, but when I came back to the kitchen, not only was my food gone, but the plate had been licked so clean, I had to check that my dinner had existed in the first place. The only proof was the dirty pots and grill in the sink. Fanny was sitting innocently in her basket and seemed outraged at my accusation of theft. Out for a walk on another occasion, she briefly buried her head in a bin liner. Half an hour later she began to retch, then I swear she regurgitated an entire, slightly green, uncooked chicken. She must have inhaled it. How she got it down her throat and back up again, I will never know.

The trick, I learned the hard way, was to have plenty of treats about my person. However distracted she was, she would focus on me the instant she heard the rattle of the treat packet. Doggy choc drops were a thing back then, and maybe she had a sweet tooth. She was mad for them and would stare at me wide-eyed, silently begging for them, straining every sinew, like a junkie at her dealer. She was a remarkably quick learner if a reward was involved. There was nothing she wouldn't do for a single choc drop. It took seconds for her to learn how to sit, lie down, stay. Once she knew I was the giver of treats, it was simple to stop her unacceptable behaviour around other foody distractions. Her early experience of starvation meant I, as the giver of choc drops, was the meaning of life. She adored me and she was lavish with her displays of affection – not just gazing at me with laser love but leaping with joy whenever I returned to the room, jumping into my arms and licking me endlessly. If I turned my head she would get her tongue deep inside my ear. If she couldn't lick my face, she'd lick my hand, my feet – even, if all else failed, a clothed limb. It was a manic, not altogether hygienic, obsession that she never grew out of. She'd lick anyone. Even strangers on the bus.

She had other habits that were just as impossible to break, and from which we must draw our own conclusions. A casually raised hand would cause her to cower, sometimes flatten herself on the floor, as if she were about to be struck. Raised voices had a similar effect: they made her assume a sort of canine brace position. Whatever traumatic experience caused this might also explain her behaviour whenever we drove along the M40, past the Heathrow Airport turn-off. Here, to allow for incoming planes, the lamp posts are low. Whenever we drove along this stretch of road, Fanny would duck at every lamp post, as if she were about to be struck. Since we were travelling at 70 miles per hour, this meant she was permanently ducking up and down, like a music fan at a 'happening' gig. Except she was clearly reliving a past trauma. I learned to try to ensure she was asleep before we drove along there.

I was enthralled by my dog. Fanny was such fun: she was bright and eager to please. She greeted everyone she met with delight and excitement. Despite what she might have been through in her past, she was never wary or shy. I thought it was important for her to have a variety of experiences as she was still a puppy, so I took her on trains, tubes and buses, to markets and shops, to parties, pubs and festivals. She was always eager and confident. She liked to be in the throb of things, always bright-eyed and curious about her surroundings. It was very rare for her to be bashful or worried.

Maybe because I was young and carefree, unaware of the risks – or possibly just reckless – I let her off the lead and didn't fret about her whereabouts. If I was at someone's house drinking, dancing and generally carrying on, as we young things did in the 1980s, I didn't give a thought to the poor dog until I was ready to leave. The first place I'd look was the kitchen, where I'd invariably find her sitting on a lesbian's lap or clearing up splashes of spilled chilli con carne from the lino floor. If she wasn't there or if I'd had a particularly eventful night, she might have sought out a bedroom or be asleep in a corner. If she wasn't anywhere obvious, I'd whistle. Each dog I've owned has had their own whistle, that has evolved to suit their personality. Fanny's was a simple two-note affair, a kind of 'Yoo-hoo!', the second note higher and shriller than the first. It worked in a park or at a party, with immediate effect. However far away she was, or however deep in slumber, she would leap up and rush to my side at once, always ecstatic to see me.

With hindsight, it all seems very irresponsible. Awful things might have happened. Fanny might easily have disappeared, been taken, come to some harm, and it would have been my fault. But I'm not here to pass judgement on myself, just to tell you what occurred as accurately as I can. It was my good fortune that fate had paired me with a dog so well suited to my frisky lifestyle. I can't say that Fanny enjoyed every moment of those wild parties but she came to no harm and had a more interesting, if less restful, life than she would have had sleeping in front of a coal-effect fire in a bungalow in Peterborough.

I spent a lot of time talking to Fanny. She would gaze at me with great interest and I'd chat away about whatever was on my mind, where we were going, who I was hoping to meet. She had an expressive face, sometimes knowing or aghast or even cynical. I'm very wary of crediting dogs with human emotions and understanding, but Fanny was exceptional. She never looked at me with blank incomprehension. Boredom, yes, and there were occasions when she'd fall asleep while I was talking, but (when awake) she always seemed to be considering whatever I was telling her and her psychic response was always one of love: unconditional love, the great gift of dogs to humanity. I very quickly became emotionally dependent on Fanny and couldn't remember my life before her. She came almost everywhere with me. We were partners, and I was never lonely with her by my side.

I've no idea why, but one day I said to her, 'You'll stay with me till I'm forty.' At twenty-one, forty seemed a lifetime away, of course. She gave me a steady, unusually mournful look. She understood the demand and the commitment she was solemnly undertaking.

'Pace yourself,' I advised. 'It's going to be a bumpy ride.'

Within weeks, Fanny understood a lot of commands (or suggestions, if you prefer). Training her was easy, as her attention was always focused on me. I learned that the best method was to wait until she was doing something, then say the command. If she happened to sit, I'd say 'Sit!' If she was walking towards me, I'd say 'Come here.' If she was getting into her basket, I'd tell her to 'Go to bed.' She mastered 'Wait', 'Freeze' and 'Walk slowly' quickly using this method: the advantage was that Fanny was given praise immediately and rarely encountered my disappointment. 'No' would stop her in her tracks whatever she was doing. 'Up' meant she had to leap in the air: I mostly used this when we were entering an Underground station and I needed to carry her up or down the escalator. From a standing position, she would leap vertically to my waist height. Then I'd catch her in my arm and off we'd go. A finger click meant she had to calm down and pay attention. It had the effect of a sedative on her. If she was told off (usually for eating something she shouldn't have), she would affect a simpering expression with hunched shoulders, half-closed eyes and quivering lips. It was so dramatic and pitiful that, whatever her misdemeanour, I would crumble at once, lavish her with affection and tell her it didn't matter.

If I was going 'out' to gay land with Steven, then Cathy or Nick would happily look after Fanny for the evening – and very possibly the night. On my return, after the ecstasy of our reunion

Fanny would sniff me disapprovingly and give me a maiden aunt look, so I'd go for a bath to wash away the smell of carnal union(s).

If I brought someone home with me, my reunion with Fanny would only last until she spied the 'trade' behind me on the doorstep. She'd sniff them, and a weak wave of her tail, the equivalent of a limp handshake, was all they would get from her. In the bedroom, as I swept dog hairs from the sheets in preparation for my one-night stand, she would jump on the chair and curl into a ball, the better to avoid seeing or hearing the congress that, in all probability, had already started.

CHAPTER 3

Fanny Feels Frisky

During these early days with Fanny, I was cheerfully unemployed. A year before I had completed a three-year Drama and English course at Goldsmiths, part of the University of London. I had arrived there a fey, virginal eighteen-year-old with a wardrobe of Marks & Spencer slacks and jumpers, and I had – as you are discovering – evolved somewhat.

Before that I'd gone to school, of course. A strict Catholic arrangement called St Benedict's, alive with paedophile monks at the time, it later transpired, although I remained untouched. The best thing to come out of my time there was my friendship with Nick Reader. He was very funny and smart, able to mimic classmates and monks brilliantly, draw hilarious caricatures and slip in and out of an array of comic personas. He gave every monk and master a nickname. I was delighted to discover that it was possible to make fun of those in authority. It had never occurred to me before.

I'd led a sheltered life in the sunny suburban streets of Teddington, where my sensitive nature and innate campness was not a concern. But at 'big school', Nick and I had some serious bullying to contend with. Life became increasingly difficult. We were nicknamed Daffodil and Daisy and became notorious for our effeminate ways and subtle rebellion. But we were best friends and together, with grace and humour, we got through.

We chose for our creed the teachings of Miss Jean Brodie, and from then on walked with our heads up, like Sybil Thorndike, 'the woman of noble mien'. I remember Nick telling the Second Master when he commented – with a spark of envy in his eye, as I recall – upon the mauve tint of Nick's hair: 'Forsooth, Mr Nickerson, I defend the right of the individual to choose the colour of his own hair.'

Our greatest discovery was Teasing Tone – a hair colourant that came in sachets, which you shampooed in. It only cost thirty pence. Subtle as they were, these colours left no one in any doubt once the wearer was sitting in one of the shafts of sunlight that shone into the school dining hall. After I had dyed my hair a ravishing Plush Peach, Nick and I were having lunch one day when a dish of tomato ketchup whizzed my way. The tide had turned, we knew. We retreated to the safety of a secret room full of old costumes from school plays that we had discovered above the stage. Little did we know then – although we were much prone to conjecture – that the events that had led to those afternoons had indicated that we were each to have a fascinating life. Even though the tide changes the detail of the shore, the fundamentals undergo no metamorphosis. Our friendship will last as long as memory.

Ever since then, Nick has been a constant in my life. Funny, arch, wise beyond his time – and unfailingly honest. As life took us down various different paths he was always there, in good times and bad, to put things in perspective. When I went to Goldsmiths, Nick went to study acting at the Guildhall School of Music and Drama.

Now I was on the dole, as were most of my friends, including my Goldsmiths graduate friends, Nick, Steven and others. Our giro cheques arrived once a fortnight and we eked out our money, living off baked potatoes and the kindness of strangers. Because we were young and full of ourselves, we assumed everything would just fall into place sooner or later.

The previous summer I had enjoyed my first 'acting' job, playing the challenging role of Aunty Vera in the Covent Garden Community Theatre production of *I Was a Teenage Sausage Dog*. It was an anti-vivisection, cartoonish show which the cast of four took on tour for several months, performing at inner-city adventure playgrounds and community centres in a cloud of dope smoke. I was on a break, hoping to be asked to do the next summer's show.

So I can see why getting a dog seemed like a good idea to me: for security and to fulfil my emotional needs. The carousel of cock I was riding was all very well, but a person needs a bit of unconditional love between ejaculations.

Speaking of matters genital, one day, when Fanny was about seven months old, I noticed that she kept licking herself 'down there'. What I can only describe as her vulva, which had always been the size of a small rosebud, was swollen and pink and suddenly of great interest to her. A trip to the vet informed me that she had come into season, which wasn't as exciting as coming into money. She was on heat. I hadn't thought about this side of doggy life before, and I certainly wasn't prepared for what was to come.

'Keep her indoors,' said the vet breezily.

With my lifestyle and Fanny's exercise requirements, this didn't seem possible. I took her to Greenwich Park as usual, and dogs made a beeline for her. As the week progressed, so did their ardour. Fanny wasn't backward in coming forward, either. Any dog with dangly bits was greeted as if she was Juliet on the balcony and they were Romeo. Never mind polite introductions, it was 'vulva in the face and let's get down to business pronto'.

As a gay man, I was familiar with the 'wham bam thank you ma'am' approach, but this was keen by any standards. We all like a good seeing-to, but my baby girl was suddenly more rampant than a coked-up rock star. Wherever she went, Fanny left an irresistible scent trail that no red-blooded male dog could resist.

After a week of this, I woke one morning to the sight and sound of six male dogs in a state of high arousal, sniffing at the front door, moaning and groaning with desire. Fanny wasn't just popular; she was Blackheath's pin-up of the month.

There was nothing for it but to retreat to safety. We got on the train to Swindon, where my parents had a secure, fenced-in garden and nothing could possibly go wrong. Or so you'd think. Unfortunately my father, getting up early to go to work as a security guard, let an innocent-looking Fanny out into the back garden at seven the next morning while I slept upstairs. Unaccustomed to Fanny's presence, he forgot about her and went off to work. When I emerged in the late morning in my Japanese kimono, there was no sign of Fanny, either in the house or the garden – until she squeezed through the fence in response to my whistle, covered in mud and with a post-coital glint in her eye. In the distance I saw a hefty black Labrador heading for the hills.

'She knows what she likes,' said my mother.

But surely she was too young? There was no way she could have got into trouble, was there? I put the matter to the back of my mind and we carried on regardless. I didn't like to think I had a child bride on my hands (the shame of it!), but within a few weeks, the thickening of her girth and the swelling of her teats told me all I needed to know. Fanny was with child.

The vet wasn't pleased. Fanny was still growing and wouldn't cope with the strains of motherhood well. He had a feel around and said it could be worse – there were only two pups there. I'd seen the size of the probable father, and was worried that the puppies would be big. Fanny's appetite – voracious at the best of times – went into another gear altogether, and I decided that the least I could do was try to satisfy her hunger pangs. I fed her four times a day and spent most of my dole money on expensive steaks for her. She was still hungry and always on the lookout for anything edible.

As the end of the ninth week approached, I made a nest for her at the end of my bed and got plenty of towels ready. The size of her belly seemed to double daily, until she looked as if she had been inflated. She could only waddle about, bow-legged and panting with effort. I felt so sorry for her and so responsible for her discomfort. She should be enjoying her adolescence and learning about doggy life, not suffering like this, her body inhabited by aliens. I rubbed her back, stroked her bulbous tummy and lavished her with affection. Food was her only comfort, so in the latter stages I fed her constantly. She was understandably preoccupied with her vulva, which blushed and grew, swelled and excreted all manner of handy slime as the day approached.

The night of the birth, she took to her nest and squatted there, panting, for several hours with a look of intense concentration on her face. I fussed about the lighting (gentle pink) and put on a cassette of comforting Louise Hay affirmations which I thought might help. Cathy was home next door, so came to look. She said Fanny would know instinctively what to do and we should leave her in peace – and put out the incense. We sat nervously on the other side of the room from Fanny, drinking gin.

It was a long night. Fanny lay down, got up again, squatted again. Her eyes grew wide with each contraction. She seemed to be struggling, but there wasn't much we could do. When she got determinedly into the squatting position again, Cathy moved forward for a closer look.

'It's happening,' she said. 'Good girl.' Just then, Fanny let out a long, anguished shriek and a glistening black, shiny capsule shot out of her – almost as big, I thought, as a rugby ball. Fanny fell forward.

'Christ,' said Cathy. 'Look at the size of that bastard!' Fanny seemed to have momentarily passed out with the strain of her exertions, then she opened her eyes and looked back in alarm at what she had produced. She licked the twitching arrival and the birth sac came apart, like cheap cling film, revealing a wet, shiny, black puppy. It wriggled towards her like a hungry Chinaman with a wok in his sights.

I knelt beside Cathy and gave Fanny a stroke as she wolfed down the afterbirth.

'It's a girl,' said Cathy, examining the puppy before giving her a rub with a towel and placing her back next to her mother.

'Enormous,' I said, a little disapprovingly.

'Imagine giving birth to that,' said Cathy. 'You wouldn't think it was possible. No wonder she screamed.'

We gazed admiringly at Fanny as she fussed over her big-boned daughter.

'I can't believe she's got to go through all that again,' I winced. But a few minutes later Fanny began to pant again and wearily got back into her preferred position. It didn't seem to be any easier the second time, and knowing what was coming reduced me to a nervous wreck. I shouldn't have had so much gin.

The panting reached a crescendo. Fanny lurched forward and screamed again, longer, louder and more blood curdling than before. This couldn't be right, surely? Another jet-black puppy shot out into the nest. Cathy helped it out of the sac and gave it a hearty rub.

'Exactly the same as the other one,' she observed. 'A healthy, hefty gal. Twins.'

Fanny looked over her shoulder and grimaced. The pups immediately attached themselves to a teat each and set noisily about their first meal.

'Oh lord,' I said, wiping sweat from my brow. 'Thank you for

your help, Cathy. I couldn't have gone through that on my own.'
I poured us both another large gin and we sat on the edge of
my bed, gazing in wonder at the two slurping beavers and their
exhausted mother, who lay on her side, vibrating slightly.

'The father must have been big,' said Cathy.

'He was, from what I saw,' I confirmed. 'And maybe all the
food and steak I gave Fanny went straight to the puppies. I didn't
think of that.'

'Thank goodness there are only two,' said Cathy. 'I don't think
any of us could go through that again.'

But just then Fanny started panting again, a now familiar look
of concentration on her tired face.

'No,' I said. 'No. The vet said there were just two. . .'.

'Blimey,' said Cathy, putting down the gin and rolling up her
sleeves again. 'I think the vet was wrong. There is another one
coming.'

Cathy was right. Distraught as we all were, we had to go
through the whole thing again. After another terrible scream,
another black female puppy, indistinguishable from the others,
was soon pushing and nuzzling at her mother, a little pink mouth
in search of a feeding station.

'Triplets!' I declared. 'The Beverley Sisters.'

But I spoke too soon. It was like we were stuck in some night-
marish, never-ending canine birthing loop. As we watched,
Fanny staggered to her feet again, panted, screamed and collapsed. As dawn began to break, the fourth and (thank the Lord)
final puppy was born. A boy this time, slightly bigger than his
sisters. With her last ounce of strength Fanny swallowed the final

placenta and collapsed onto her side, blood on her lips. Her poor, ragged vulva pulsated and glistened in the morning light. She managed a little water as I slipped the bloody towel from under her and her brood and replaced it with a clean one.

Cathy and I finished off the gin and lit ourselves a well-earned Benson & Hedges.

I'm not sure the trauma of that night ever left me – or Fanny, who had, after all, done all the hard work. My attitude to the pups was soured. While I looked after them with care and did my duty, even now, forty years later, whenever I think of them I see blood and hear Fanny's screams ringing in my ears.

That morning I looked at the four helpless, suckling newborn pups and saw only a gang of parasitic brutes: heartless, ruthless and insatiable. I'm not sure that Fanny's opinion differed from my own. She fed them and cleaned them and perhaps felt a certain pride in their robustness, much like Violet Kray felt towards her troublesome twins, Ronnie and Reggie, but beyond the instinct to feed and protect them, I'm not convinced she was infused with motherly love.

We named the pups Molly, Margaret, Harriet and Wesley. You could just about tell them apart, if you could be bothered: Molly had a white front paw, Margaret had a white flash on her chest, Harriet had slightly wiry fur and Wesley was blessed with a penis. But they didn't, at this stage anyway, have discernibly different personalities. They were just a collective of ravenous thugs. I'm sure that, if Fanny's milk had dried up, they'd just have helped themselves to a limb each.

Two days after they were born, Fanny was ready to go for her usual walk in Greenwich Park, her nipples red raw and swinging in the breeze. She seemed in no particular hurry to get back home to her babies.

It only got worse, of course. Eyes opened, claws and teeth grew, legs became stronger. Fanny took every opportunity to get out of their reach, if not out of their company altogether. By the time they were three weeks old she would feed them standing up, back arched like a cat, wincing with pain as they devoured her with their razor-sharp milk teeth, while needy, high-pitched squeals of dissatisfaction filled the air.

At three weeks, the pups were getting adventurous. They were old enough and bold enough to explore the rest of my room, outside the cardboard box. They were still constantly at the breast whenever Fanny appeared, but I did my best to relieve her, buying a product called Lactol and introducing them to solid puppy food too. This meant poo and pee in abundance. They didn't seem to sleep much, either. If they weren't defecating or emptying their bladders, they were yelping, playing, wrestling or chewing something they shouldn't be. The situation was only going to get worse, so I called my parents. My father came up to London in the Zephyr and transported us all to Swindon, where the puppies could wreak havoc in their new garage accommodation and frolic in the garden. Fanny took to the lounge with an apologetic look on her face, and had to be sent into the garage three times a day to feed them. I went with her to hold her paw as the Hounds of the Baskervilles chowed into her like something from a horror film.

By six weeks we'd all had quite enough, and we found suitable homes for all four. The afternoon they left, great relief swept over Fanny. She didn't whine or go looking for her children. She gazed at me thankfully as I bleached the garage floor, and the unseemly business of her teenage pregnancy was never mentioned again. The only reminder was her poor teats, which dangled, chewed and elongated, like chewing gum, for some months.

In due course Fanny went to the vet to be spayed. We couldn't go through that again. Besides, life was about to get quite busy.

CHAPTER 4

Camping in Kidbrooke

In the summer of 1982, I was summoned back to Covent Garden Community Theatre to do another kids' show called *Aaaaargh! No! It's 'Orrible!*, which was about the evils of germ warfare. Being a nice, liberal, lefty company, no one had any problem with me taking Fanny, either to the rehearsal room or on tour. Fanny would sit and stay, either in the church hall or minibus, until told to do otherwise. Her only lapse was when another company member's dog – Tess, a Welsh border collie – was around. Tess would incite Fanny to misbehave and play chase, which is your only interest if you're a Welsh border collie. I think Fanny only joined in to be polite.

As for the show, it wasn't the best entertainment ever created. Mainly because the director (not to mention the cast) smoked a lot of dope and never got around to writing the ending. Audiences, assuming we had paused for a scene change, were surprised to see us loading up the van, ready to leave – quite hurriedly, as we had joints to roll. Our dope smoking was prolific: on the way to a gig, before and after. Sitting in the van with us chuffing all around her, Fanny's good behaviour might, in retrospect, be put down to the fact that she was stoned too.

Then, in the autumn of that year, via a friend of a friend, I was drafted in to replace an unsatisfactory actor in another curious production, called *Chase Me Up Farndale Avenue, S'il Vous Plaît*. Entertainment Machine were well known in fringe circles for their chaotic pastiches of amateur dramatic shows, in various genres, be it Shakespeare, murder mystery or science fiction. Regular characters added continuity, such as the Queen of the Farndale Ladies Amateur Dramatic Society, Phoebe Reece. How I came to be cast as this provincial middle-aged dragon at the age of twenty-two is lost in the mists of time, but it was great fun. As Mrs Reece I had such memorable lines as: 'Those of you with gramophones may be interested to know that the live cast album of *The Mikado* will be on sale in the foyer after the show. Mr Cheshire, who did the recording, apologises for the traffic noise, but he couldn't get the bedroom window shut.'

We opened in the Isle of Wight after three days of rehearsal then toured the UK, finishing, as you do, in Milton Keynes. Luckily Fanny loved all the travelling and the constant stimulation of new towns, digs and dressing rooms – not to mention the frolics and parties after each show. She'd settle in a corner watching us dance and gurn into the small hours then squeeze into my sleeping bag with me, sighing contentedly. She licked away the salty sweat from my face with endearing enthusiasm, and if she ingested a little recycled stimulant this way, it didn't seem to affect her.

Some dogs are child substitutes, but Fanny was more of a parent substitute. You may think from my account that I was behaving like a drug-addled slut, but without Fanny's watchful gaze it might have been a lot worse, believe you me. People down on their luck who you see sitting on the pavement outside supermarkets often have a world-weary-looking dog with them – most often of the Staffie variety. This may be a marketing ploy to encourage dog lovers to give generously, or it may be that the dogs are much-loved guardians, preventing their master or mistress from slipping into more wayward habits.

Certainly that was the case for me. I was having a high old time – in every sense. My own recreational drug-dabbling days were in their infancy in the early 1980s. There was more to come. I look back on it now from my abstemious sixties and it all seems fairly harmless, in the context of the time. Who wasn't enhancing their evening with a little sniff 'n' spliff? No one, in my circles.

Fanny was the perfect non-judgemental companion. She would stay awake all night with me and sleep all day if that was what I needed to do. She'd be gentle and affectionate if I was in a delicate hungover state, and accompany me to the the next party with a cheery wag of her tail when I was ready for another round of debauchery. Thank goodness things like crystal meth weren't around then for me to experience. Oh, wait – I'm afraid there is a story about that coming up in Part Three. Sigh. Drugs are like bicycles, don't you think? In the 1980s you didn't see anyone on them and they were quite gentle and benign. Nowadays they're everywhere and might well kill you.

If things got a little too hectic, Fanny would happily go and stay with friends. I would hand her over and she'd trot off without a backward glance. An actor chum, who took her in more than most and who wisely has decided to remain anonymous, has this recollection:

She was, of course, an absolute people-magnet/tart – wherever you were with her, people would stop to stroke and talk to her: her sweet, small frame, those deep, kind brown eyes, velvety ears and Queen Mum-like brown teeth were irresistible, it seems. She was always very accepting and generous with her cuteness and time for them.

I have to confess that once, and only once, I exploited her powers of attraction. I was with her at a fairly late hour walking past that tea-bar that stood outside Waterloo. There was a very acceptable chap who caught my eye buying a tea and, you know, suddenly I had a yearning for Typhoo as well, and joined the queue. Somehow, Fanny got tangled in his legs. I was apologetic, and the guy immediately went down for a stroke – and then we drank our teas and gradually, almost wordlessly, in the fabulous way that things worked in those days, we moved to the idea of 'going on somewhere', al fresco, which seemed very exciting. We headed down that street with the garage under the arches, which was full of old Citroëns that were used for filming, and in a very gentle sense got slightly better acquainted. Fanny stood guard. Afterwards I can honestly say that I never felt judged by her – though of course she could be very private with her thoughts.

Of course, let's face it, it was nothing she hadn't seen before.

Around this time, Fanny and I experienced some changes to our domestic arrangements. Cathy was hanging up her nurse's uniform to get married and have babies, and I was offered a hard-to-let council flat in Ridgebrook Road, Kidbrooke, in south-east London. 'Hard to fit into' would have been a better description, but the thought of a home of our own was rather appealing.

The flat consisted of one room with a toilet (no bathroom as such) by the front door opposite a 'compact' kitchenette. The novelty was the bath, which was under the kitchen counter. I slept on a fold-out sofa. The other novelty was the surly youths who populated the estate – they must have thought it was Christmas when an effeminate actor and a dog called Fanny arrived in their midst. They took to gathering near my block and crowding around us when we ventured out, hissing unpleasantries and clenching their fists. Fortunately, I'd dealt with this kind of carry-on at school so I was able to defuse things before they got physical, with a tried-and-tested formula involving imperious indifference, wit and the occasional flirtation.

Fanny, clever as she was, didn't understand homophobia. Because of the wide range of words she understood, I could string together 'downstairs', 'toilet' and 'hurry up', and open my front door. She would take herself off to the grassy area to the side of the block, do her business (you didn't pick up poo in those days) and come back to the flat. She'd slip through the gang and shamelessly do her business before their very eyes.

One of the gang, a lanky youth with the looks of a young Ethan Hawke (well, if you half-closed your eyes) presented himself at my front door one afternoon holding a bucket and asked if I wanted my windows cleaned. I only had two windows. I hesitated. Should I allow a homophobe inside my flat? But my windows were dirty so I said yes. Fanny eyed him suspiciously as he set to work with a sponge and chamois. I heard a familiar metallic rattling sound and looked up from my book. The window cleaner had turned away from the window, his belt buckle undone and his flies open. He stared at me darkly.

Fanny pricked her ears up, sensing a change in the atmosphere. I could have grasped the pink oboe of opportunity – but I didn't. A horny window cleaner presenting himself in this way may be a gay fantasy come to life for some of my readers, but you'll be surprised to hear that I rolled my eyes and returned to my Muriel Spark novel. I wasn't in the mood. He hadn't bought me a drink first. He had BO. And I'd been around the block enough times to know that for men confused about their sexuality, a sudden rush of post-orgasmic guilt might cause him to lash out at the object of his desire. He tidied himself up, I paid him and he left without a word.

It was an advertisement in the back of *The Stage* newspaper that led to my next job. I became a singing telegram. They don't exist now – a bit like phone boxes and Tupperware parties. But in the 1980s no classy social gathering was complete without either a busty girl doing a strippergram or someone like me (or more butch) dressed as Tarzan turning up to surprise the birthday girl – or boy – with a jungle-inspired song and a banana.

It was difficult to get around from Kidbrooke, so when the

telegram agency offered me a little Honda van, on the condition that I also delivered helium-filled balloons as required, I said yes. Fanny sat on a pile of cushions in the passenger seat and off we went. I would deliver three or four telegrams a day to various locations – anywhere from a posh house party in the suburbs to a crowded pub in the City. I'd wear my loincloth under my jeans, so it was just a question of stripping off once I'd parked, tousling my hair and getting to it. If it was a 'standard' job, Fanny would wait in the van while I sprinted to the location, found my target and returned. If a 'deluxe' telegram had been booked (it cost an extra £7), I was required to stay and get the party going for twenty minutes. Fanny would come with me then, Cheetah to my Tarzan, happy to be fawned over by the revellers, especially if there were crisps going.

I've always been happiest when I've felt self-sufficient. The singing telegrams era ticked this box perfectly. The agency would call me with my bookings for the day, I'd slip on my loincloth, stock up on bananas and off I'd go. Once a week I'd go to the agency and get my money. It was quick and easy and I made people happy. With Fanny by my side and an *A to Z* on the dashboard, I whizzed around London feeling like a free spirit. I'm drawn to low-brow culture. I watch *Love Island*, not *The Sopranos*. I read true crime books, not Nabokov. I like mongrels, not Crufts Best in Breed. To find myself singing a saucy song in a crowded pub, with my nipples on display and Fanny as my assistant, was a curious turn of events, but one I found unexpectedly fulfilling. Of course, at the time I didn't think, 'I wonder if I could spend the next forty-odd years doing something along these lines?' It is only in hindsight that I can see this as the beginning of all that was to follow.

Me singing a tuneless version of 'I'm the King of the Swingers' wearing a leopard-skin thong in the Gladstone Arms in Bermondsey in 1983 is not a million miles removed from my version of 'Wandrin' Star', which I performed, dressed as a giant party popper, in the Palladium panto in 2018. Fanny waited in the van in 1983, Albert waited in my dressing room in 2018. Same nonsense, really. Funny how things turn out.

Also around this time, I was introduced to the curious world of fringe venues – pubs mainly, but also vegetarian cafes or tents at little mini-festivals – where 'alternative' performers took to the floor (there was rarely an actual stage). Andy Cunningham, the director of the Covent Garden shows I'd been in, also performed. He had an act with a puppet called Magritte the Mind-Reading Rat, and I went along with Fanny to watch. (Later Andy would achieve success at the BBC with his act rebooted as Bodger and Badger.)

Anything might happen at these evenings and anyone might jump up and perform: comedians, singers, poets, ventriloquists, mime artists. With Fanny sitting on my lap I enjoyed these evenings, but I felt a flutter inside. It would be even more fun to do a turn myself, surely? Andy encouraged me, and with a friend called Chris Stagg I cobbled together ten minutes of material. A few weeks later at a venue called the Earth Exchange in Highgate, I made my debut as Gillian Pie-Face, wearing a blonde bubble wig and a black and silver kaftan. There was no place for Fanny to wait so I took her on with me and handed her lead to a member of the audience to look after. With remarkable foresight I kept the script, some of which I can now reproduce for you word for word:

My name is Gillian Pie-Face and I'm a qualified agony aunt and a feminist spiritualist healer. I've leapt off the page this evening to come and deal with my public on a one-to-one basis. I've come to get to grips with your emotional needs and to bathe your wounds with my very own sponge of sympathy. . .

I read out some letters, sifted through the audience looking for those most 'in need', and the act culminated in one poor unfortunate man receiving the laying on of hands. In a way, this was an advanced evolution of the singing telegram. The name wasn't right and neither was the 'auntie' image. My love of Dame Edna was perhaps a little too evident. But something about Fanny sitting watching me with rapt attention gave me an idea. At the next gig, I carried her on with me and sat her on a chair. 'This is my Fanny.' I noticed the audience seemed much more attentive having the novelty of a dog to look at, and Fanny sat upright, enjoying the warmth of the stage lights, looking calm and serene. Good-natured heckling was commonplace and welcome at these shows, and that night a man at the front tried his luck. I forget what he said, but I remember Fanny's reaction. Sensing mild aggression, she glared at him, outraged. The audience laughed.

'You might not think it, but she is a Rottweiler,' I informed him. Fanny stared at him for the rest of my act, never blinking, like a bouncer averting a ruckus in a nightclub with a steady, warning look. My applause at the end of that night with Fanny on stage with me was much warmer and longer than I had come to expect. Maybe I was on to something?

CHAPTER 5

Fanny Learns her Trade

Eventually, alternative comedy had its own weekly listing in *Time Out* magazine. Generally, the door takings were split between the performers (£10 each was above average), but sometimes you'd just get a free drink or a plate of food for your trouble. Several of the acts ran their own nights in rooms above their local, and performers made bookings either through friends or word of mouth. My only requirement was a bar stool on stage for Fanny to sit on. I took choc drops on with me. I established that it wasn't easy to catch one in your mouth by throwing them at the audience, thus ensuring applause when Fanny caught one with nonchalant ease.

Dynasty was my favourite programme at the time. After watching a particularly gripping episode, I was inspired to change the name of my act to the Joan Collins Fan Club. It was a 'eureka!' moment and I instantly knew I had found my niche. I made a cup of tea and, with Fanny sitting next to me on the fold-out sofa bed, I scribbled down the torrent of ideas that were swirling around in my excited mind. The wig could go, and the kaftan too. There was no need to assume a female identity either. I didn't want to impersonate Joan Collins, but as her Fan Club, I'd naturally assume all the carefully groomed style, bitchiness and ruthlessness of her persona. It was the New Romantics era – I could present myself as a glamorous man. A gay man. Why not? It would be bold and shocking. Through acting as a fervent admirer of Joan, I could adroitly comment on her ravenous media domination and steely determination to succeed. There was comedy gold to be had there, surely?

The idea of making myself dazzling and alluring in the setting of dingy pubs was thrillingly incongruous. It was also unique – in their effort to escape the sexist, racist image of mainstream comics from the 1970s, all the other comedians were deliberately dressing down. Well, Paul Merton was wearing pyjamas on stage and Steve Edgar wore a bow tie, but no one was getting dolled up in quite the way I intended to. Plus, I had a performing dog! She needed a title too. I stroked Fanny and looked into her eyes. The Amazing Fanny? Incredible? Wonderful? The Wonder Dog . . . the Joan Collins Fan Club with Fanny the Wonder Dog. Was it too long a title? No. It was perfect.

I experimented with a few different looks – glitzy, ill-fitting outfits from charity shops, with stilettos and feather boas. I even acquired a couple of dusty old capes from a retired drag queen in Lewisham, but nothing seemed quite right until I saw someone wearing rubber at a fetish club in Soho one night. I knew this was the way forward.

I went on stage at my next gig wearing black rubber shorts and vest, with black and white striped tights, patent leather Doc

Martens, a pink sequinned garter on my thigh, a studded dog collar around my neck – and Fanny tucked under my arm. Joan Collins has always been generous in her use of make-up, so I trowelled that on, too. And then some more. Black eyes, beauty spots and red glittery lips. It's fair to say that I stood out among all the jeans and T-shirts.

There was still something of the agony aunt about my new material. I read out a letter, supposedly from a childless couple in Wandsworth asking for Joan's help, which launched me into an account of Joan's latest venture, the JCFC Surrogate Mother Foundation. I seem to recall that the foundation was desperately short of sperm donors and, as I explained to the gentlemen in the audience, I had placed some receptacles in the loos, should any of them feel the need to leave me a small deposit.

'Don't worry if there's a queue. That can't be helped. It's really a case of first come, first served, and I'm quite sure that if we all pull together I won't leave here empty-handed.'

I kept the singing telegrams job going alongside the cabaret work. The gigs started rolling in – not due to my more alluring appearance, but because the alternative cabaret circuit was growing fast. Fanny, meanwhile, was remarkably consistent in her stage-craft. She sat, pert and bright-eyed, on her stool and caught the choc drop I tossed her way every time with ease. Fanny had stage presence. But, lovely though she was, it was clear that the audience wanted more from her than a game of catch. How could I utilise her charisma in the interests of light entertainment? The answer came one night when I stood side-stage listening to a young Rory Bremner perform. (Rory wore tight trousers in those days, incidentally, and the rumour, confirmed from my vantage point that night, was that he always performed with an erection.) Maybe Fanny could do impressions? There was a thought. But how and of whom? It might be funny if she didn't really do much. It would all be in the eye of the beholder. With a few props, perhaps? Yes, more like a naff game of charades. The audience would have to guess who or what she was trying to convey.

I thought about this over the following week as I drove to my Tarzan-o-grams. One day when we were stuck in traffic, I leant over to Fanny to do one of her favourite things: whisper in her ear. She loved being whispered to – lips against her ear, soft, private, conspiratorial words. She would close her eyes and very slowly raise her head until her nose was pointing to the sky. When the whispering stopped she remained in that position, eyes like slits, as if in an altered state of consciousness. The traffic eased and I drove on with Fanny in her Zen-like state. Then I had an idea for her final impression.

The following Friday I was booked at an alternative comedy evening in the back room of a pub in Lewisham, the Amersham Arms. It was here that Fanny's impressionist skills made their debut. As if I knew the stars were aligned, as I left home that evening to go to Lewisham I grabbed my ghetto blaster. It would be fun, I suddenly thought, to have some music to enter to, rather than the usual smattering of unenthusiastic applause. There was no sound system in the pub's back room, so I would take my own. The cassette that happened to be in the machine that day was a compilation of famous movie themes. Perfect. I would mince on to 'Tara's Theme' from *Gone With the Wind*.

What with the music, my shiny black rubber get-up and Fanny on her stool next to me, the audience were interested before I said a word. We did the choc drop routine and I launched into my patter about the JCFC Surrogate Mother Foundation. I chatted to the audience for a bit, was rude about their clothes and hair, and then it was time for the new bit.

Fanny's looking a little restless. I think she'd like to do her impressions for us now. I'll just give her the cue. There. She's gone into the first one now. [Fanny's demeanour hasn't changed in the slightest.] I think the eyes give it away. It is of course . . . Jack Russell Harty.

They do get better. Now who's this? [I lift Fanny's paw and wave it about. Lean my face into her so she licks my ear.] She's waving at you and she's kissing me. That's a dead giveaway. Pope John Paul the Second. It's uncanny, isn't it?

The third one. [I hold some plastic fruit on top of Fanny's head.] Any ideas? It's Canine Miranda!

Next. [I lift up Fanny's gums to reveal her brown incisors.] The Queen Mother!

Who is this? [I put a red wig on Fanny.] Fergie!

Now, a well-known film. [I switch the wig for a green battle helmet.] *The Dogs of War!*

[The helmet is replaced with a shower cap.] Yes? *Psycho!*

A well-known pornographic film which no doubt many of you have at home on video. . . [Fanny catches another choc drop.] That's *Deep Throat!*

She is artistically drained now, but she has energy for just

one more. . . [I whisper in Fanny's ear and she slowly raises
her head.] That is . . . *Tower Bridge!*

We were a hit. That was the night when everything came
together and fell neatly into place. The Joan Collins Fan Club
with Fanny the Wonder Dog evolved from that night on and
other opportunities began to present themselves. If we enjoyed
performing in dingy, smoky venues, well, there were plenty of
those to be found at the Edinburgh Fringe . . . so why not go for
a sniff round there?

CHAPTER 6

Fanny Loses Interest

For our first Edinburgh Fringe in 1985, Fanny and I teamed up with two acts from the circuit, the droll Jewish comedian Ivor Dembina and a musical double act called Skint Video, comprising Steve Gribbin and Brian Mulligan, who sang energetic pastiches of current songs, with the words changed for comic effect. For example, the Smiths: 'I would go out tonight, but I haven't got a vegetable to wear.'

We played in a basement bar called the Abercraig Lounge beneath a chip shop on the corner of Broughton Street and Picardy Place. I needed a changing area, so was allocated a disused kitchen on the ground level. I laid my make-up out on the stove and Fanny curled up for a pre-show nap in my suitcase. I was staying in a room in a vicarage, shared with my old chums from the Farndale Ladies, who were there doing a show called *The Revenge of the Really Big Men*. The three weeks went well, and I squeezed in lots of extra shows at the Fringe Club and other cabaret clubs.

I got on with my fellow performers, but found them a tad

blokey. Fortunately, during these years – her prime – Fanny was always ready for life's adventures. She sprang into action every morning and looked at me, bright-eyed, eager to find out what the day had in store. A trip out to friends, a party, a gig, a wander through a graveyard – she was happy to go anywhere and loved meeting new people and experiencing new places. Her natural friendliness was a good counter to my own standoffishness. I have always been a little wary when among strangers, and there's nothing quite like a small mongrel jumping up on laps and licking faces to break the ice.

So all was well at the Abercraig Lounge, but I couldn't help feeling there was more fun to be had, on stage and off. I made a mental note that, for the next festival, I should maybe choose my fellow performers myself. The show might be less random, more satisfying. We could all interact more instead of being confined to twenty-minute slots. I wanted my own gang. It didn't seem too much to ask.

My hunch proved correct.

I met Barb Jungr and Michael Parker in 1985 on the circuit and much admired their set of beautiful, blues-inspired songs and harmonies. They were quirky and fun. Barb in particular, with her raucous laugh and determined quest for fun, was great company.

Another comedian, Steve Edgar, was handsome and stylish. His comedy was an account of his 'acts of mischief', such as putting a lone pack of Jaffa Cakes among the washing powder in supermarkets, or being personally responsible for *EastEnders'* Wicksy's annoying hit single. 'I did that' was his catchphrase.

Fanny took a real shine to Steve and would sit on his lap at every available opportunity, which was perfectly understandable.

Barb, Michael, Steve and I got together and without much difficulty conceived a show that we called *Fourplay*. We all had our own slots but there was interaction and collaboration. Best of all, some songs we did together as Fanny sat patiently on her stool and listened.

As Barb recalls now: 'We had a fantastic festival: we swanned round in a big group and always seemed to be in exactly the right place at the right time. If there was some fabby party, we were there. We were Julian's gang and we had a great time.'

Barb isn't wrong. With glowing reviews and our three-week run selling fast, we were in the mood to party every night after our show, and the jolly times continued back at our large, shared flat. If I fancied a spot of sporran I'd leave Fanny in Barb's care and slip away to gay land, safe in the knowledge that they'd all still be awake when I got home. There were gales of laughter from my room one morning when the man I had enticed back revealed the words 'SUCK ME' tattooed on his penis.

'In case ye cannae understand ma accent,' he explained. Like I'd need telling.

Happy days indeed. I love Scotland and all Scottish people, with the possible exception of Dennis Nilsen.

Our success followed us back to London, and *Fourplay* was booked as a job lot for some more gigs. The fashion for singing telegrams evaporated as quickly as it had arrived and I had to manage without the Honda van. This meant taking a late-night train back to Kidbrooke after work, followed by a perilous mince through the estate with only Fanny for protection. This was unsatisfactory, but the happy synchronicity that has always blessed my life came into play and changed everything. I received a letter from the Seymour Housing Co-operative, inviting me for an interview. I had placed myself on their waiting list a while back when the situation with the local youths was particularly trying, but had then forgotten all about it. A week later I sat before the panel, Fanny on my lap, and made my case. I wasn't homeless but I was being victimised because of my sexuality, and my work meant lengthy journeys late at night. They looked sympathetic, but it was Fanny's pleading, watery eyes that swung the interview in my favour, I'm sure of it.

A few days later I was offered a studio flat – no bigger than the one I was in but with a proper bathroom – in a smart red-brick block built around a charming courtyard garden, a short stroll from Baker Street. My postcode was to be W1, not SE something or other. And I could walk to most gigs! It was bliss. And I credit this moment as the one when everything began to change.

I didn't know for sure – how could I? But I could feel it in the air.

When writing about my life with Fanny in the 1980s, it would be easy to erase the darker moments, or simply omit to mention them. But I was in my mid-twenties and far from immune to self-doubt. While I was doing okay, determinedly pursuing my life as a cabaret performer, I didn't, up until this point, know where it was leading or what was to become of me. I sensed that my family worried about my future, and expected me to 'settle' at some point and get a proper job. I was well into my twenties, after all, and the main relationship in my life was with Fanny the Wonder Dog. By twenty-eight my parents had three children and a mortgage. What was I doing with my life? Was it not time to think about these things now?

The person I would turn to for rare bouts of self-analysis was my old school friend Nick. He had given up acting and was working as a chef in a pub in Soho, where the proximity to booze was proving hard to resist. When drunk, he was vicious and outrageous, capable of clearing a room in minutes with vile, deadly observations about people he'd only just met. But when sober he was as perceptive and wise as ever, and could reframe a situation or dilemma with a pithy quote or calming interpretation of my situation: 'As Muriel Spark puts it, one's prime is elusive. You must be on the lookout to recognise your prime at whatever time of life it may occur. You must then live it to the full.'

Maybe Nick was right, I thought. Maybe this was actually my prime and I just hadn't recognised it yet. In 1985, on my first night in bed at Flat 21, Seymour Buildings, Fanny tucked in her usual position, breathing contentedly, her back pressed against my chest, I could sense something intangible: a fuzzy vibration in my limbs, a chattering of my guardian angels, perhaps, an aligning of the planets. Who can say? It was a feeling of safety and well-being. Something good was happening. This feeling stayed with me the next day as I took Fanny for her first walk in Hyde Park via the subway at Marble Arch. Here I found a much better class of dog walker and more exotic dogs than Kidbrooke had to offer. I was more likely to be cruised than insulted, it seemed. As we strolled along, I dreamed up some new nonsense for the act. Performing at the Edinburgh Festival meant that new material was required annually, so new routines or 'sections' were constantly occurring to me.

During the move I had discovered I owned a life-sized sponge puppet of a man with a grinning face. I had acquired it after one of the Covent Garden Community Theatre shows. This gave me an idea. At my next gig, I took the puppet on stage with me and introduced him as Vick the Veg, Latex Stud. He was the main feature of the JCFC Fun Pack and came complete with the JCFC Relief Lotion (the crystallised remains of the scum off her bath water, scraped from the enamel of her Hollywood bath and jarred for your convenience) and JC's Vanilla Disco Rub, which doubled as a dessert topping or a lubricant: 'Think of the fun you could have at the tea table – or indeed under it. . .'.

This new routine required me to carry more props around – Vic needed his own suitcase – but he was soft, so when he was propped up in the corner of a dressing room Fanny made herself comfortable on his spongy lap. Joan Collins – along with the Princess of Wales – was the most famous woman in the world at that time, and the idea that she was endorsing a multitude of products and making money out of anything she could seemed like a jolly comedy ruse. I just needed to take it to ridiculous extremes.

I finished my act by telling the audience all about the soon-to-be-opened Joan Collins School of Acting for Stage, Screen and Airport Terminal, which allowed me to make plenty of digs at some of the less talented thespians of the day. It seemed to go down well.

The novelist and wise woman Fay Weldon writes: 'There seems to be an overall pattern in most lives, that nothing happens, and nothing happens, and then all of a sudden everything happens.'[2] This seems to be true of my life. Having bobbed along on the cabaret circuit for five years or so, I was then asked to appear on Channel 4's *Saturday Live* in February 1987. As a consequence of this, everything happened and everything changed. In those days a single TV appearance could alter the course of a career in an instant.

Suddenly I started to be recognised while I was out and about. Without the make-up and the rubber I was fairly incognito, but Fanny was instantly recognisable and always gave the game away. Of course, she loved being fawned over by all and sundry whenever we stepped outside Seymour Buildings, but our progress to the park or supermarket was rather hindered.

Our TV appearance had been a success, Fanny's impersonations were a hit with the wider public, and we were invited back on *Saturday Live* two weeks later, where we did a sketch written by Paul Merton and me, in which I was dressed as a (glittering) police constable with Fanny as my sniffer dog. We were elevated to star billing at future gigs and we were being circled hungrily by agents and TV executives.

This was all fascinating to me, and rather exciting. It was what I'd hoped for, but I hadn't thought it through. How could I? I'd been happily plodding along, a self-sufficient turn, amused that I could get away with being paid for talking nonsense, and eyeing up the next steps on the ladder as they came within my reach. But over the next couple of years, those rungs would fly past with unseemly haste. This would change not only the way I worked and where, but also how people treated me. They treated me better, on the whole, but – and I barely noticed it at the time – an authenticity began to evaporate. Sincerity became hard to gauge.

There is a certain light that shines in people's eyes sometimes when they encounter a famous person. It might be from the thrill of the encounter – or from the horror of it. From the recipient's point of view, it can be hard to tell. It may manifest as obsequiousness or disdain. Ordinary encounters with strangers are never the same. Friends may be pleased for you, or cynical. What would previously have been a cheery chat might be a minefield where they compare their circumstances to yours, leading to awkwardness. And no doubt, as I went through this process I, too, behaved differently: I may have been self-important or self-doubting, but I was also self-protective. It was complicated. And all the time I knew it was too late. I had settled into my carriage on the runaway train and it was accelerating. I might as well enjoy the ride.

Besides, it all changes over time. You go from 'I hope this person doesn't recognise me and ask for an autograph' to 'Why don't they recognise me? Have I been forgotten?' quickly enough, as last year's winner of *The Voice* will tell you. I'm happy to report that this all evens out in the fullness of time. By the time you get to my age, you can only concern yourself with your own thoughts and responsibilities. Other people's expectations and opinions are of minor interest. When I think back to all the energy I wasted on feeling inadequate and anxious, I get quite cross with myself. Luckily for everyone around me, I always had a dog beside me to stop me tipping too far over the edge into the celebrity trap and the misery found therein.

But I may be getting ahead of myself here. Fast and dizzying as the changes in my life were, there were other, more mundane, matters to deal with first. Expectations were now high in all directions, although not all of them were to be fulfilled.

It was just as well that I'd come up with new material a few months before – I was going to need it. At that year's Edinburgh Fringe, it seemed a good idea to do a show on my own, which meant filling a whole hour, rather than the usual twenty minutes. Songs were a good idea, but that year Jungr and Parker were working with Arnold Brown in a show called *Brown Blues*, which went on to win the prestigious Perrier Award, so I plucked a talented pianist called Russell Churney from obscurity. With some new songs, the Joan Collins nonsense, Fanny's impressions, and a new *Dynasty* audience-participation ending that I had written with Paul Merton's help, I just about scraped through. In truth, I was a bit short – but as long as I found someone to pick on in the audience, I could fill the time.

The problem was keeping Fanny's attention for the duration of our allotted spot, as I found out on our opening night. She was all bright-eyed for the first ten minutes and thrilled to be the centre of attention, but we still had fifty minutes to go. Trouble arose when Russell and I went into an ill-conceived number about a paedophile relative titled 'Was That a Robin I Saw Bobbin' on your Finger, Uncle Tom?'. She glazed over. To be fair, so did the audience. Like an elderly aunt nodding off at the dinner table after too many sherries, Fanny's eyes slowly closed and her head lowered. I tried to jolly her along with a few extra choc drops, but I was fighting a losing battle. Curling up for a proper snooze wasn't possible on the bar stool, so after a yawn and an uninterested glance around, she jumped off the stool and began to wander around the audience looking for crisps, pulling focus from the musical entertainment we were attempting.

Fanny was old school, clearly. Twenty minutes was her limit. She wasn't going to sit there like a lemon while I floundered around endlessly. The next night she did her bit then looked at me knowingly. I went with the flow. 'Fanny is exhausted after her endeavours and needs a lie down in a darkened room, ladies and gentlemen.'

She left the stage to tumultuous applause. Less is more when you're the star turn.

That was the beginning of the end for Fanny's performing days, I now realise. I had always thought there was something distasteful about performing animals in circuses or elsewhere. Tigers on podiums, elephants holding each other's tails, poodles wearing tutus and walking on their hind legs didn't do it for me. But Fanny was only really on stage by accident. Because she wanted to be with me. She liked the warm lights. She sat and caught choc drops and I pretended she looked like the Queen Mother. As the circuit, and our presence on it, got larger, so did the audiences and the stages. There was more pressure for me, and no doubt dogs absorb this from their owners, whatever the circumstances. There was a big difference between twenty minutes on a makeshift stage in the back room of a pub a couple of times a week and hour-long shows in 'proper' theatres night after night. What if it wasn't fun for her any more?

I pushed this thought from my mind. After all, Fanny was only showing signs of boredom. I wasn't subjecting her to an electric cattle prod. Nevertheless, as soon as our stint in Edinburgh was finished I took Fanny on holiday with my parents to Cornwall for a well-earned rest.

My new manager, Addison Cresswell, a cheery faux Cockney geezer with an intense manner, offered me a rather sobering contract in which he promised to 'represent [me] in all [my] activities throughout the world in and connected with every aspect of the entertainment industry including but not limited to performing and recording, writing and composition, publishing and merchandising activities'. For a camp comic and his dog who until very recently had gladly performed in exchange for a plate of brown rice and lentils, this was quite a leap. I asked if a handshake would suffice instead.

'No problem, Mush,' said Addison. Fortunately, Fanny liked him. As many a gentleman caller had discovered, if Fanny didn't signal her approval (by licking them), then there would be no second date.

Addison called me late one night and babbled on about photo shoots, magazine covers, TV shows and fifty-date 'major' tours. I tried to take it all in. He had great plans for me. For all I knew, it was just talk, but as things turned out he had the talent and determination to make it all happen. But before I was exclusively 'his', I had a few more gigs in the diary which I had to honour.

One was in Newcastle. Fanny and I caught the train there. It was delayed for some reason, so I was in a fluster when I got out of the taxi outside the venue with only half an hour to spare. As usual, I told Fanny to wait on the pavement while I struggled with the bags and suitcase. She sat down, wearing her usual patient expression. I turned my back for a moment to pay the taxi driver, who had seen us on *Saturday Live* and was complimenting us in an incomprehensible Geordie accent while I nodded at what I hoped were appropriate moments, when I heard the screech of brakes, followed by a deadly thud and a distressing canine yelp.

I turned to look for Fanny, but she was no longer on the pavement.

CHAPTER 7

Love and Loss

I stood on the pavement of Collingwood Street, frozen with fear. Ten seconds earlier she had been sitting behind me. What had happened? Why had she moved? Why hadn't I held on to the lead? Just then Fanny staggered into my line of vision from the road, and I swept her up into my arms. She was trembling, but I could see no blood. The taxi driver helped me carry my bags into the club. Fanny must have – somehow – bounced off the car that hit her. In the dressing room I stroked her and comforted her and, with a shaking hand, put on my make-up.

I know. It was not appropriate. I should have cancelled our appearance. I should have found a vet and had her examined. She might have sustained concussion or internal injuries. What made me think the show had to go on? It was only a small basement gig; I wasn't depriving thousands of clamouring fans. I can't explain my thinking; I can only record the facts. Maybe I was in shock myself. I put my slap on, squeezed into my rubber shorts and carried Fanny onto the tiny stage. Decades later, I still feel guilty about that night. Ever the pro, she caught the choc drops and we got through the act, but I could see the terror in her brown eyes and see her trembling. I cut things as short as I could and got her back to the quiet of our B&B.

Not surprisingly, Fanny's enjoyment of being on stage faded fast after that. We had one or two more attempts, but waves of terror washed over her from time to time and she'd look at me with pleading eyes, clearly imploring me to get her out of there. The fun tends to go out of things, I find, after a near-death experience. I finally behaved like a responsible dog owner and decided Fanny was to retire. Addison wasn't best pleased. I had just recorded a single of the Shangri-Las' song 'Leader of the Pack' and was soon to embark on a tour of the same name. Artwork of me on a motorbike with Fanny had already been printed and 'WITH FANNY THE WONDER DOG' was written in large red letters.

'It's the dog people come to see, mush!' he said between expletives. But short of finding a dog therapist to rekindle Fanny's love of being on stage (and I don't think they'd been invented yet), there wasn't much we could do. Fanny was retiring and that was that. But she was still going to come on tour with me. She would wait contentedly in the star dressing room and have her own minder to keep her company. We reached a compromise whereby Fanny followed me across the stage, trotting briskly from one wing to the other, glancing casually over her shoulder at the delighted audience. For this she would get rapturous applause.

But that was it. Fanny never lingered on stage again. She would sit beside me on chat shows, pose for photo shoots and make cameo appearances on future TV series, but her days of pandering to the public and being a 'turn' were behind her. As always, her timing was perfect. Her sudden withdrawal from public life made her much more famous than she would have been, I suspect, if she'd carried on until the public had had their fill, her whiskers were grey and her coat had lost its sheen. She retired when she was at her most beautiful, like Greta Garbo. People were clamouring for Fanny the Wonder Dog, but Fanny said goodbye.

Today, it's well over thirty years since Fanny shunned the lime-light, yet people still remember her and ask after her, whether I'm in Marks & Spencer or the VIP lounge at Auckland Airport. She is frozen in time in people's minds, still that frisky dog with knowing eyes.

'She was a star,' said a man in Regent's Park the other day. So maybe that's the explanation. You might toil away in a popular soap for years, be a one-hit wonder with screaming fans for a while, but when your star fades and you're earning a crust selling burgers in a lay-by, you are forgotten. Not so for Fanny. She just sat on a stool and caught choc drops while I put some silly props on her head, but to some people she is a legend.

But although she wasn't to be part of the act any more, Fanny still had a lot of living to do. And as TV work came my way, I made sure she was represented on screen. *Sticky Moments* was a riotous parody of tacky game shows conceived by Paul Merton and me as a vehicle for my penchant for insulting members of the audience. The set, designed by Anne Tilby, was a witty mash-up of Chagall-esque shapes and pictures of Fanny were everywhere, from giant cardboard images hanging from the ceiling to stylised

Fanny brooches made of plastic resin which we gave to every audience member. The winner of the show was given a ceramic effigy of the Wonder Dog's elegant head to hang on their wall. Fanny herself appeared briefly in one episode, sitting on a chaise longue next to me while I sang 'You're My World'.

After the first two lines, in which I extoll the elevated position she occupies in my life, Fanny had heard enough and left the studio, leaving me to gaze lovingly at the empty sofa, as I sang about her paw resting in mine, bestowing a power so divine.

We did a book too, *My Life With Fanny the Wonder Dog*, which Paul Merton and I wrote in a few weeks, locked away in an office in Percy Street. Since Paul was involved, we didn't feel too constrained by the facts and were free to veer off into fantasy as and when we felt the need. To set the tone, my bio on the back page informed the reader:

Julian is a carefree individual who loves life and life loves him. His great passion is, of course, mountaineering. In 1981 Julian was the first man to mince up the Matterhorn. A year later he climbed the difficult north face of the Eiger in slingbacks.

The text was lavishly illustrated with photos by Peter Mountain, and luckily Fanny had no objections to the three-day shoot. The book was just the start. My life had changed considerably in the few months since Addison became my manager, with tours, live videos, TV, corporate gigs and more. The first big TV show I was involved in was a Saturday-night ITV game show called

Trick or Treat with Mike Smith. It wasn't a great success but after twelve episodes it elevated me, if that's the correct word, into the mainstream, and my brazen image caused a certain amount of highly enjoyable outrage. Fanny's presence softened my in-your-face gayness, but some people considered me a threat to conventional family values, and possibly the very fabric of civilised society. An article in *Marxism Today*[3] (where else?) put it rather pleasingly, I thought:

> His is the last laugh on a TV culture tired to death of being so safe and so straight. If Julian can be popular, what hope is there for an endless schedule of bland quiz shows on deregulated TV? He's now well placed to brighten up a wet Sunday on the box.

But working on *Trick or Treat* taught me a valuable lesson: I needed more control, otherwise there was a distinct possibility of disaster. I didn't fit in to conventional television formats, and being told what to do by old-school TV types was irksome. Addison understood this. At the time, it was all the rage to form your own production company, so we did this. Wonderdog Productions was our name, and a photo of Fanny catching a choc drop was our logo. Television series such as *Sticky Moments* and *Terry and Julian* were produced from our little office in Noel Street in Soho, where Fanny and I spent most of our days. The shows we made were much more my kind of thing, made by a team who bought into my world and enjoyed breaking conventions. The producer Toni Yardley and director John Henderson created a stress-free environment that allowed me to be relaxed and think on my feet. Witty costumes by the talented Michael Ferri and beautiful make-up by Michi Nakao helped the non-sense along in the right direction, too.

Then there was all the money that was suddenly coming my way. I had to register for VAT, Addison informed me, posting me the forms to sign along with the cheery message: 'You are now part of the elite band of rich bastards earning £20,000 or more a year . . . Jeremy Hardy, Arthur Smith, Harry Enfield. Need I say more?'

My raised profile had also prompted a delightfully minty letter from Joan Collins' lawyers informing me that 'Miss Collins wishes Mr Clary the best for his chosen profession but will not accept that he should pursue it by wrongful association with her name and reputation.' That was fair enough, I suppose. The time had clearly come to use my own name. I'd been thinking as much anyway.

The only disadvantage to being in the money was my living arrangements. I never thought I'd leave the safe haven of the Seymour Housing Co-op, but it was social housing intended for those on a modest wage. The blacked-out Mercedes parked outside waiting to whisk me off to the TV studios was a little incongruous. It was time for us to move on. Sad as I was to leave, my pay rise meant I could buy somewhere with a garden for Fanny. We had only ever lived in flats and I was accustomed to late-night and early-morning trips around the block. Imagine the convenience of simply opening the back door for her ablutions! I started to look for a new home.

You might think, with all that was going on, that my love life was on hold. Let me reassure the anxious reader that I wasn't going without. Far from it. Like all homosexuals, I require sex every twenty minutes – and on Fridays I'm on a twenty-four-hour loop with just a thirty-second break to catch my breath. I was making hay while the sun shone. Enough hay for several haystacks, if you get my meaning. If we were on tour we'd always sample the gay clubs in whatever city we found ourselves in. Fanny would be looked after in the hotel by the straight tour manager. (Heterosexuals have their uses, after all.) If I was in London, well, gay life was there on my doorstep and it would be churlish not to round off the evening with a trip to Heaven, Bang, Stallions or wherever. Fanny would look my conquests up and down with weary resignation when I got home in the small hours, then go back to sleep. If I hadn't tired of them by morning, they weren't dysfunctional, had no personal hygiene issues and they hadn't wet the bed (you'd be surprised), sometimes we'd round off the encounter with a dog walk in Hyde Park. And that would be that.

Then one night I met Christopher at a club called Paradise in Islington, and everything changed.

Christopher was handsome, with dark hair and sultry eyes and an air of amusement about him. The music, noise and smoke of the crowded dance floor seemed to melt away until it was just us two gazing at each other, as if we were alone on the top of a misty mountain. Scents of jasmine and rosemary filled the air and I could hear the distant chanting of Tibetan monks in my head. We laughed and kissed and I clung to him as if I had discovered a much-treasured item in a lost property office and had no intention of mislaying it again.

When we got back to Seymour Buildings, Fanny greeted him like a long-lost friend. I thought he must have treats hidden about his person (I wasn't wrong there. . .). This good omen proved to be telling. Fanny's character judgment was spot-on. Christopher was worth wagging your tail for, and we were an ideal match. Without really thinking about it, we started a relationship. When he was with me, things were more fun, the sun shone more brightly and life seemed to be smoother and more exciting at the same time. Fanny even got into bed with us, which was unheard of.

We were shy, though, and the greatest faux pas on the gay scene was to declare yourself or appear needy in any way. We kept things strictly casual and our dignity intact. But of course, the truth will out: love will show itself with a look or a touch, whether the host likes it or not. Christopher came to my shows, met my friends, and we spent our weekends together. The months flew by in understated bliss, with my career and love life in perfect harmony for once, it seemed.

Then one Friday night he didn't turn up for our date. I called him several times over the next few days, but his flatmate said he wasn't there. This sort of thing isn't unusual in gay relationships. Our attention spans are very short and there are so many other fish in the sea. I had to face the fact that Christopher had moved on with bewildering suddenness, and endeavoured to do the same myself. I had been so sure of him, so it was extremely painful to have to reassess the situation and return to single life.

There was a wistfulness about me for the next six months that didn't go unnoticed by Fanny, who upped my licking quota and gazed at me with loving sympathy.

Christopher's return to my life was dramatic. One night I woke to an urgent knocking on my door. Fanny's excited greeting, jumping and licking rather got in the way of Christopher's slurred declarations of love, tears – and then some other news.

Fanny sat on his lap, her eyes shining with delight. Christopher stroked her back and rubbed her chest as he explained his absence. He had been in hospital with pneumonia and had since been diagnosed with full-blown AIDS.

I opened a bottle of wine.

Christopher was like me; he didn't like serious talk. We found it irksome and embarrassing. Perhaps we were too cowardly to confront his grim prognosis, perhaps the delight we felt at being together made illness and death too incongruous to contemplate, or perhaps we were just too young and optimistic to think such things might come to burst our bubble, so in the spirit of Scarlett O'Hara we decided to think about it all tomorrow. No amount of talking or contemplating would change anything, after all.

A few months later, when I moved into my newly purchased ground floor flat in Camden, complete with a petite walled garden, Christopher did too. We didn't discuss that either; it just happened by osmosis.

This was the start of a new era in Fanny's life, in several respects. Showbiz life was a distant memory for her. The unfortunate incident in Newcastle had put an end to her stage performances but now, with Christopher at home, she didn't have to sit in tour buses or dressing rooms either. Christopher had stopped work (something to do with computers. I didn't ask and he knew better than to try to tell me). Like a husband off to work in a 1950s sitcom I would kiss wife and child and they'd wave me off to a hard day's graft. When I got home, they'd be curled up together on the sofa.

They were besotted with each other. I felt the odd twinge of jealousy, especially when Fanny switched sides of the bed, preferring Christopher's spooning to mine. Christopher walked her, fed her and kept her amused. Gone were the dubious selection of men I used to drag home, that would mean her ejection from the bed for the night. I was settled with Christopher and she was reaping the benefits in her middle years. A hint of grey was appearing around her chin and her running in Regent's Park was not as athletic as it had been in Greenwich.

Fanny, of course, was oblivious to the elephant in the room: the disease that we all pretended wasn't tightening its grip. She ignored Christopher's persistent cough and slept through the sheet changes that were necessary when he had night sweats. If the arm that encircled her at night was a little bonier than it had been the previous year, or the face she licked had sinister red blotches hidden with Hide-the-Blemish, it didn't seem to matter to her.

When Christopher had to stay for a few days in hospital for procedures that neither he nor the doctors seemed to understand the benefit of, she welcomed him home with ecstatic leaps and licks. He promised he wouldn't leave her again. If Christopher needed to stay in bed all day, she was delighted to join him. She watched with a curious expression as he rattled his many pill bottles and popped pills in his mouth, much like she had with choc drops in her heyday. But now there was no applause, only ponderous silence until he opened the next bottle and made his selection.

We were determined to be happy, blinking back tears when we had to face the sobering facts spelled out by plain-speaking doctors. Our response was always to run away – we recklessly went on holiday to New York, Portugal, the Maldives. Medical insurance didn't enter our thoughts. I don't regret those eighteen months of self-denial, of refusing to face facts. Our happiness was real, as was our love. We didn't face the future because we knew, as far as being together went, we didn't have one. Like the gay community of which we were a part, there was something of the Merry Widow about us. Fear and grief might be all around, but fuck it – there were parties to go to and people to meet, even if they were pale and thin and not long for this world.

When Christopher didn't come home from his final visit to hospital, Fanny looked at me with sad, questioning eyes before walking slowly into the garden where she lay down in a patch of sunshine. She lowered her head on her paws and gazed at the wall. I like to think there was a whiff of Greyfriars Bobby about Fanny that day – the famous Skye terrier who spent fourteen years guarding his owner's grave until Bobby died in 1872 – but this may be fanciful. She slept on Christopher's side of the bed that night. She didn't eat for two days and didn't want to go out for a walk. We kept apart. We moved around in silence, sometimes stopping halfway across the room, as if we could not think and move at the same time. Then on the third day she came to me, slid quietly onto my lap and gave me one solitary long, gentle lick.

CHAPTER 8

The Wrong Move

Fanny appeared alongside me in a couple of scenes in the sixth episode of the Channel 4 series *Terry and Julian* in 1992. She sat next to me as Terry (played by Lee Simpson) and I chomped our way through a mountain of breakfast cereals.

'That's another one done,' says Terry. 'I must say, this has turned out to be a marvellous hobby. Entering competitions.'

'I've enjoyed it,' I agree. 'Mind you, it's Fanny and I who have to get all the coupons. My mouth has been full of crusty bits since last Thursday.'

'Stop complaining. You'll be happy enough when we win something. Now, let's see. I've done Spot the Ball,' says Terry.

'So have I,' I say, quickly feeding Fanny more Coco Pops, as she is clearly getting restless.

'Guess the Pope's equivalent weight in paperbacks,' Terry continues. 'And we stand the chance of winning a Volvo if Petula Clark turns out to be an anagram of apricot.'

'Who wants a Volvo?' I mutter. I then have to go off-script as Fanny looks as if she is about to jump off her chair. 'Stay where you are, please!' I tell her. 'You! Don't look at me with those accusing eyes.'

It was clear that Fanny wasn't happy when I wasn't paying her attention, so I directed the next bit of dialogue to her instead of Terry. 'Complete the following quotation, Fanny, in ten words or less, and you could win a luxury holiday for two in Spain.'

On the recording, you can hear Fanny's high-pitched impatient whine.

'What's the quotation?'

'I like KY jelly because. . .'.

'I like KY jelly because. . .' Terry ponders.

'I like KY jelly because . . . a pack lasts the whole weekend. Unless you bump into the Lowestoft rugby team, then who could say? I wonder if we'll win?'

But for the last few lines, a tighter shot was used in the edit: Fanny had departed.

A few scenes later we are on a flight to Spain. Fanny is sitting restlessly next to me as we order fancy cocktails from the flight attendant. Terry orders a tequila sunrise.

'And for you, sir?' asks the trolley dolly.

'I'll have a Greek youth in a pair of Y-fronts, please. Make him a large one.'

Fanny has a similar 'get me out of here' look on her face as the flight experiences some turbulence. I do my best to keep her happy, surreptitiously feeding her biscuits, but it is a losing battle.

'All the blood's rushing to my head!' complains Terry.

'This is no time to get an erection,' I caution him. I'm holding on to Fanny as she attempts to jump down from our seat.

'Much more of this and we'll be seeing my complimentary nuts again.'

There was a big laugh coming up and I wanted to get to it before Fanny got her way and escaped. 'I hope the pilot's all right. Mind you, I could always help him out. I'm experienced in these matters. Once when we were in Tangier I brought a jumbo in single-handed.'

'Doesn't surprise me.'

'Those Moroccan terminals are a tight squeeze.'

But during the above dialogue, Fanny went. She could stand it no longer. It was to be her final television appearance. Even though people were thrilled to see her, she was clearly experiencing some anxiety and wasn't enjoying a second of it. I was adamant that I wouldn't put her through it again. Fanny was officially a recluse.

Since Christopher's death I had more or less elected to carry on regardless, and news of my 'secret heartache' had – mercifully – been kept out of the papers. I had commenced writing *Terry and Julian* with Paul Merton in the Wonderdog office the day after Christopher's funeral, in fact. Paul was sensitive and understanding, as well as hilarious company. Just the ticket under the circumstances. I'd also completed a live tour called *My Glittering Passage* with Barb Jungr and Michael Parker, with Russell Churney on piano and my glamorous assistant, Hugh Jelly.

We finished the tour in style at the London Palladium and my heart swelled with a moment of joy, despite everything. I also found time to film *Carry on Columbus* at Pinewood Studios.

All of these light entertainment endeavours had been scheduled before anyone knew I was going to be bereaved, of course, and with my star in the ascendant it seemed a shame to cancel anything. For what? So I could sit at home and be miserable? Surely making people laugh was a form of therapy in itself?

But looking back, that time seems a little manic. Anyone would think I was taking vast amounts of cocaine to cope with the workload. Ahem.

The only thing I had done, which I knew at the time was a mistake, was to move home again. To Holloway. No one moves to Holloway unless they are a little off-kilter, believe me. Maybe the grimness of that area of north London chimed with my subconscious. Who can say? I knew the day I moved in that it was a mistake. The detached house was big, gothic and miserable, with bad vibes. Fanny grimaced as I walked her up the garden path for the first time. It was nowhere near a park or any green space, and she clearly hated it as much as I did. She also went deaf overnight, as if she didn't want to engage with me any more.

Then, a month after I'd moved house, my friend and old cruising companion Steven died. AIDS, once again. I say it brutally, and why not? It was too monstrous a thing to stare in the face; I could only respond by shrugging and carrying on. Those of us that the lottery spared, who were allowed to live, owed it to our departed friends and lovers, I felt at the time, to live lives worth living. We had to live for everyone. The incongruity of being a gay comic at the time of a gay plague was enough to curdle the spirit if I paused to think about it. So I didn't. What I think now is what I thought then: I must press on with the rest of my life. No good will come of too much loitering.

Add into the mix piles of prescription drugs from a well-meaning doctor, and a psychotic cat called Gloria who would lie in wait for me in the dark then attack, and you can see I was set to spontaneously combust.

The tinder was the 1993 Comedy Awards, at which I was making an appearance, and the spark was the presence of the then Tory Chancellor of the Exchequer, Norman Lamont. He was in any leftward-leaning person's bad books for saying, 'Rising unemployment and the recession have been the price we have had to pay to get inflation down. That price is well worth paying.' I had nothing left to lose, so I went for it. Glancing at the bucolic stage set I said: 'Very nice of you to recreate Hampstead Heath for me. As a matter of fact, I've just been fisting Norman Lamont. Talk about a red box.'

Cue much tabloid newspaper outrage – and, it was predicted, the end of my career. I didn't much care. I was holed up in hideous Holloway in a Valium daze with Fanny looking curiously at me, as if I were a stranger. For the first time, she took to sleeping in another room, avoiding my toxic presence and messy unravelling.

When you are sad or unwell, it seems to me, dogs can display concern and sympathy: they sit with you and empathise. But druggy self-medication or psychotic behaviour is another matter. All my dogs can spot a 'mad or dangerous' person at a hundred yards, and their reaction is to alert and protect me. When Christopher was ill, Fanny hardly left his side. My reason for being unhappy was understandable, but my reaction to the circumstances – the downward spiral of self-destructive behaviour, pills, alcohol and self-pity – was not. Fanny elected to remove herself from the situation as far as she could. Her 'get me out of here' expression returned. A display of canine tough love, possibly. Or maybe she had absorbed some of my malaise and was miserable herself.

Anyway, I didn't overdose or check into the Priory or give up showbiz and become a recluse. I had some counselling with a man who never spoke, just nodded sagely and looked at his watch while I worked through my feelings, which clearly weren't as interesting as I thought. I weaned myself off the sleeping pills and sedatives which had been so moreish, and realised that my recreational drug use was not helping my recovery. I had sleepless nights, cold sweats and dark thoughts. My friends devised a rota system of care and concern and love, then one night I felt the familiar thud of Fanny landing on the bed beside me and I knew that all would be well.

I also moved out of the house of horrors, put everything in storage and went on a tour of Australia and New Zealand with a new show called *My Boyfriend's Back*. I always recommend a trip to Australia to any disgraced celebrity. Australians genuinely didn't understand what all the Norman Lamont fuss had been about, and replayed the moment on Breakfast TV when I was being interviewed.

While I was away, Fanny had a well-deserved break from me and went to stay with my parents in Swindon – a holiday of a lifetime, as I'm sure you'd agree. There she could play with my parents' two cavalier King Charles spaniels, Bonnie and Zara. Mind you, I'm not sure how much fun this would have been for her: cavaliers are so mind-numbingly dull that playing might be too advanced an activity for them. They are best suited to blinking. Which is a good way, incidentally, to tell if they are still alive. Zara died one night of a suspected heart attack. My parents stepped over her until lunchtime before they realised she'd 'gone'. From the look of boredom on Fanny's face when I got back, I surmised that it must have been like spending six weeks with Andy and Jamie Murray.

The Comedy Awards incident follows me around like a bad smell, of course. Nearly thirty years later, it's rare for the matter not to be brought up in an interview. On radio or daytime television they wince slightly, wanting to cover the territory of my disgrace but anxious that I don't use the word 'fisting' and get them taken off-air. Like a lot of people, my parents didn't understand the mechanics of this niche sexual practice ('The act of putting a fist in an ass or vagina, very popular practice among evolved [kinky] gays. Requires great care and huge amounts of lubrication' – Urban Dictionary). Although my name is synonymous with fisting – spoiler alert – I've never felt the need to try it myself. Not that this has stopped me from demystifying it for my audiences during live shows, should it come up in conversation. The silver-haired ladies of Harrogate were particularly stony-faced, as I recall. I can't think why.

CHAPTER 9

OAP (Old Age Pup)

When I returned to the UK I set about buying a new home back in Camden, which I should never have left. I find Camden a pleasing, thought-provoking mix of nationalities, age groups and social strata. There is a jauntiness about the place, a middle finger to respectability, a brightness that infuses the lucky inhabitants, whether they live in a hostel or a Georgian townhouse.

I chose a house on a busy street, because I like to look out of my window and see 'goings on'. A leafy side street where cats stare at you and curtains twitch wouldn't suit me. I like a bit of background noise: cars, passers-by, drunk people and the occasional fight. I'm near the park, a corner shop, the high street, a Japanese restaurant and a gay pub. Bliss. (Well, the gay pub, the Black Cap, has closed. But the ghost of Regina Fong lurks inside and God help the property developer who tries to turn it into swanky flats. She will haunt them relentlessly until they give in and return it to its rightful purpose.) It's also a safe Labour seat, which is important to me. I need to know that the person in front of me in the supermarket is a like-minded socialist. When I pass through Chelsea or Kensington I glare at the smug Tory-voting inhabitants and have to restrain myself from shouting abuse at them. I'm so left-wing I frighten myself sometimes. In fact, if I wasn't a camp comic and renowned homosexual I'd grow a beard and wear corduroy. That's how left-wing I am.

My mental equilibrium returned as soon as I was settled in the house, where I still live. The panic attacks that were such a feature of my malaise still pop up occasionally, like Jim Davidson on the telly, but, just like Jim's appearances, I have learned to breathe through the distress and ignore them.

Fanny was happy too. Happy but still deaf. Dogs don't seem to be aware of their own hearing loss, and she was overcome with surprise if I came in and found her asleep on the bed, mortified that she hadn't heard my key in the lock and welcomed me with her customary greeting ritual of jumps, wags and licks. Over the next couple of years she became almost completely deaf and oblivious to my cheery chatter. (Not as distressing as you might think, apparently. My current husband claims he sometimes leaves his earplugs in for the whole morning to give himself what he calls 'respite' from my inane commentary.) Slowly, sign language took over. I'd have to clap my hands to get Fanny's attention, then give her a range of visual signals that she understood:

Patting my lap – come and sit with me.

Point at her basket – go to bed.

Exaggerated wave – I'm off out.

Arms flapping up and down (used in the park, mainly) – come back to me.

Hand to ground – I've got something for you.

Pointing to wet patch on carpet – you've had an accident.

Kneeling on all fours – come and lick me. (NB: This works with men, too.)

Despite her deafness, her favourite thing was still to be whispered to. She would press the side of her face to my lips while I uttered sweet nothings into her ear, she would assume a posture of deep, meditative pleasure, and she would stay in this position for as long as I kept up the gobbledegook. At night she still slept in bed with me in her usual position, and she liked to fall asleep to my murmuring.

She slept a lot more than she used to. Slept and snored. Her limbs got stiffer and she preferred a gentle meander to running or jumping when we went for our daily constitutional.

Despite the tabloid predictions, I still had plenty of TV work. In the spirit of change I'd also acquired a new agent: Mandy Ward at International Artistes. Fanny would either come with me to the studio and rest in the dressing room, a runner tending to her every need and (if at the BBC) taking her to the Blue Peter Garden for a tinkle, or stay at home with a selection of dog-sitters. This was a much-coveted role. She was still recognised when we were out and about, but this was mercifully still the pre-selfie era, so the public weren't quite so 'in your face' about things as they would become.

All Rise for Julian Clary ran for two series on BBC2 from 1996 to 1997. It was set in a courtroom, with me as the judge, resolving real-life and not-very-important disputes for people, such as neighbours forcing a green-fingered friend to enter the Croydon in Bloom competition against his will, or a case of slander between a vegetarian and a meat eater. You get the idea – it was just an excuse for me to insult people from the provinces, really.

'You remember Rumpole of the Bailey? Well, I'm more rump than pole. . .'.

The court was guarded by two steroid-guzzling hunks and the clerk of the court in series one was the wonderful Frank Thornton, who we called Geoffrey Parker-Knoll.

'How are you, Geoffrey?'

'Like a good stilton, I improve with age.'

'I'm more like a Marks & Spencer Jersey Dessert. I need eating by Thursday or I'll go off.'

Frank wasn't available for the second series, so my new clerk was the inimitable June Whitfield, playing Auntie June: 'This may come as a surprise to everyone, but my nephew Julian is a bit of a one for the ladies.'

'Yes, well, the lighting's better there than in the Gents.'

It culminated in a Christmas special.

'I don't know about you, but I'm laying on something special this year. I thought maybe a Gladiator. But it's the stuffing I enjoy most. Then, if I've got any room left, I like to get my lips round a yule log.' I assure you, it's what the public wanted at the time.[4]

Sky TV was viewed with some suspicion when it started up, but it had lots of money and decided to spend some on a new 'fun' series called *Prickly Heat*, (1998–2001) which I co-presented with Davina McCall. It was filmed on the beach in Magaluf in Mallorca and involved four teams of skimpily clad boys and babes competing in 'madcap' games. These involved gunge, balloons, slides and stuffing an octopus down your briefs. Think *Love Island* meets *It's a Knockout*. As we sheltered from the heat in our air-conditioned Winnebago one afternoon between takes, Davina told me she'd signed to do a new series called *Big Brother* for Channel 4.

'It's going to be huge!' confided an excited Davina. I didn't like the idea of it and advised against. My judgement in TV matters has always been dubious. When Paul Merton told me about *Have I Got News For You*, I was similarly sniffy: 'I wouldn't do a panel show if I were you. It'll never last long. Say no without hesitation.'

Luckily for them, they ignored my advice. I was team captain on a BBC1 quiz show called *It's Only TV . . . But I Like It* (1999–2002)⁵. I didn't much, but I managed to film four series. It was no great chore. It was filmed on a Monday evening, and I just had to get to the BBC in the afternoon, peruse a script in my dressing room while Fanny snored on the day bed, then mince into the studio and make a few withering comments. The finished product was, like lots of TV, the sort of thing you might have on in the background while attending to something more interesting. Like cutting your toenails or looking at brochures for camper vans. Jonathan Ross hosted, and Phill Jupitus was the rival team captain. As the title suggests, the show was all about television, past and present.

Jonathan: 'What a week in TV it's been. We've all been trying to work out who shot Phil Mitchell. Phill Jupitus thinks it was Tamzin Outhwaite, while Julian's fingered Martin Kemp.'

It wasn't groundbreaking, but some iconic TV personalities were on the panel with me. I met Valerie Singleton, no less, and fulfilled a lifetime ambition by being in the same room as Claire Sweeney, about whom I have an unsavoury obsession.

I filmed the first of four ITV pantos in 1998, whetting my appetite for the 'real thing' a couple of years later. I am very glad I did my TV stint at the time I did, when wages were generous and budgets were sizeable. There was money for posh sets, make-up artists, designer suits (shoes, shirts, even cufflinks), after-show parties and top-notch catering. Afterwards you'd get a kind letter from the producer thanking you for your contribution. Those days are gone, I can tell you. Now, I know I'm not the hot property I was – I'm lukewarm and cooling fast – and I hesitate to bite the hand that (once) fed me, but I was recently asked to appear on a TV show for nothing. Wear your own clothes, do your own make-up, get yourself there and home again, and bring your own sandwich. Do it for the exposure, no questions asked.

There has always been a higher quota of cunty types working in television than in other walks of life (with the possible exception of the Catholic order of Benedictine monks), but I suspect they have been breeding among themselves because now the studios are overrun with ruthless, glassy-eyed types who don't know how to smile and whose mission in life is to get as much out of you for as little outlay as possible. And don't even think about taking a small, well-behaved dog with you to sit in the dressing room (if you have one) while you fulfil your duties. To do this, you'd have to fill out copious health and safety forms weeks in advance and even then the work experience runner will have forgotten to tell Security, who'd greet you at reception as if you're a convicted paedophile with a bound, gagged Boy Scout thrown over your shoulder.

But I digress. And breathe. . .

After filming the first series of *Prickly Heat*, I spent my earnings on an apartment in a charming Mallorcan fishing port called Puerto Andratx, where, as it happens, my sister Frankie has lived since the early 1980s. There I could have lots of happy times with her, my nephew and nieces, friends and relatives. I was also in the habit of catching taxis late at night to Palma, where, if you drank enough Carlos Gran Reserva Brandy de Jerez your night would go with a swing and no mistake, although you might not remember the names of everyone you met the next day . . . Like the man who lured me back to his place one night then appeared the next evening in the port, serenading diners with Spanish love songs on his guitar at the waterfront restaurant where my mother and I were dining. I gave him a generous tip, which he received with a knowing wink.

In the meantime, age had tightened its firm, sinewy grip on Fanny. Cataracts made her eyes milky and dull, and arthritis meant her once elegant trot was reduced to a creaking shuffle. Her coat didn't shine any more, but became dull, powdery and speckled with dandruff. I'd had a dog flap installed so she could take herself off to the garden for her frequent visits. One afternoon there was a terrible, prolonged clatter and crash. I rushed to see what had happened. Fanny lay in a heap by the back door, having tumbled head over heels from the top of the stairs to the bottom. Nothing was broken, but she was bruised and dazed. After that I either carried her down to the garden or walked in front of her.

She was still endearingly affectionate. She slept in my bed as she always had, even if I had to lift her on and off, and I didn't mind the copious moulting or the toxic old-dog breath that could strip paint or kill a canary. Talking of smell, that became the only sense she had left, and she utilised it to the full. Our shuffle around the park consisted of me waiting patiently while Fanny found aromas of exquisite interest in every blade of grass.

Fanny managed a brief walk-on part in a 1998 TV special called *In The Presence of Julian Clary*. Her appearance, if we can call it that, before a celebrity audience that included Phillip Schofield, Dora Bryan, Peggy Mount and the Beverley Sisters lasted about ten seconds. I regret it. She just stood there, looking dazed. 'She wanted to show you that she's still alive. Riddled with cystitis,' I told them.

I wanted to put 'the life span of dogs' into Room 101 when I was a guest on the show of the same name in 1999. As I explained to the host, Paul Merton:

> I just don't think it's fair. You get this lifelong companion, as Fanny was, and is, and you invest a lot of feelings in this dog and then you watch them get old before your eyes. Then they die at some point and you have to grieve. Fanny is eighteen now and she can no longer stand. She can walk into a room and she has to find the nearest wall. She leans against the wall, then you can see the back legs go so she has to sit down, then she pretends she wanted to sit down all along.

'She's eighteen, but in dog years that's something like a hundred and thirty-three,' Paul said helpfully.

'I know. I can't bear it. She is the living dead. I think she's just hanging on for my sake. I got Fanny when I was twenty-one. It would be lovely if you could choose your dog and they could grow old at the same pace as you do.' I was exaggerating Fanny's frailness for comedy purposes, but I stand by my objections to a dog's relatively brief life span. It's too cruel.

As Paul O'Grady says, 'To invite a dog into your life – or any animal – means you inevitably invite heartache. But then, why contemplate the hangover when you're at the party?'

But you could argue that old dogs are wise and can teach us compassion, patience and gentleness if we let them.

Gloria the vicious cat was in her prime. I had seen a notice in the vet's when I first moved to Holloway and took pity on her. I shouldn't have. She was demonic and short of an exorcism there wasn't much to be done about it. Gloria was well aware of Fanny's compromised reactions, she took great delight in lying in wait for her behind a door or on the landing. When Fanny appeared, Gloria would spring out with enviable sprightliness and cuff her around the face. Fanny got so used to this, she would wince in anticipation whenever she entered a room. The vet examined Fanny and said she had a strong heart, so until something else gave out she would go on and on. And so she did.

Fanny's judgment of my gentlemen callers wasn't always so reliable as she got older. Take Luciano. Tall, dark and handsome, with enough body hair to stuff a king-size mattress, Luciano was, he told me in stilted English, an Italian professional basketball player. Fanny was fascinated by the scents she found on his clothes and hair, and wagged her tail and sniffed him from top to toe the moment we got home. To my human nose, his aromas were unusual, which I put down to pheromones. Or perhaps Italian food and sweat from his exertions on the basketball court. I was surprised when he asserted that he was not gay, given that we had met in a seedy club, but we had a nice chat and a cup of tea.

I didn't think I'd ever see him again. But I was wrong about that. I had recently had some tasteful calling cards made, with my name and phone number and a classy gold border, so before he left I casually gave him one. Every few months, out of the blue, Luciano would call. Over a crackling line from whatever country he told me he was competing in, he would say, 'It is me. How are you? How is Fanny?'

Sometimes Luciano would announce that he was in London and so, much to Fanny's delight, he would visit me in Camden for a drink, always followed by the announcement that he wasn't in any way gay.

'Of course not,' I'd reassure him. 'The very idea!'

The unusual smell of a straight man never lost its allure for Fanny. Luciano's arrival was always greeted with the snuffling enthusiasm normally reserved for Fortnum & Mason's top-of-the-range dog treats.

The friendship continued for a year. I never knew when he'd pop up, as it were. I once walked out of the stage door after a show at the Leas Cliff Hall in Folkestone and there he was, asking for a lift back to London. Fanny and I almost fell out over who was going to sit on his lap for the ride home.

Then one day something unexpected happened. I was in the middle of a photo shoot when I had a phone call from the police. They wanted to come and see me as a matter of urgency. What was it about? The detective couldn't say over the phone.

The next morning the long arm of the law arrived at my house and introduced himself as Detective Inspector Horrocks from Scotland Yard's Kidnap and Specialist Investigations Unit. He opened his briefcase and placed a 10×8 mugshot on the table.

'Do you recognise this man?' he asked.

I did.

'That's Luciano. He's an Italian basketball player,' I said.

The detective inspector raised his eyebrow. 'Is that what he said his name was?' he said with a shake of his head.

Turns out that Luciano wasn't called Luciano, he wasn't Italian, and he certainly wasn't a professional basketball player. His name was something quite different, and he was a Bulgarian people-smuggler. You could have knocked me over with a button mushroom. He was well known to the police, having been arrested several times for being here illegally. No sooner was he sent back to Bulgaria than he would return. The police had found my calling card in his pocket.

Things began to fall into place: the fascinating smells Fanny had inhaled weren't Italian food or perspiration but shipping container, rubber dinghy or the smell of human fear.

Months later, I had a message on my phone from the ruthless Luciano. 'Sorry' was all he said. But that was all he needed to say. A few years later, it transpired that I had reason to thank him. He sold the story of his people-trafficking life to *The Sun* newspaper, who printed a front-page story under the headline 'MAFIA PLOT TO KIDNAP CLARY'.

Ruthless maybe, but definitely not gay. It was too good a story not to use on stage, so I did. I wrote a song, which I still sometimes perform.

> *You're really not Italian,*
> *You're really not what you say.*
> *You're really not coming to terms with the fact*
> *That probably you're gay.*
> *Probably you're gay.*
>
> *If you wear paisley underpants,*
> *If you think* Top Gear *is great,*
> *If you don't take it up the arse,*
> *Then probably you're straight.*
> *Probably you're straight.*

While all this was going on, Fanny was spending increasing amounts of time at my parents, who were both retired. Life was steady and calm there and she wasn't subjected to Gloria's muggings or random appearances from fake Italian basketballers. At my parents' house, she would take herself for a walk around the house, through the French windows, past the rockery, down the side of the house and in through the back door. She would repeat this circuit over and over, her head bobbing purposefully, until she was gently interrupted with a biscuit and encouraged to rest. I didn't think the end would ever come.

That spring my friend Penny, who was one of Fanny's favourite dog-sitters and who had changed career from being an actress to an intuitive healer, called me out of the blue to say that she was getting strong psychic urges and wanted to see Fanny 'to say goodbye'. I was so resigned to Fanny's end-of-life phase that it took me a while to realise that it might be Fanny who was to depart, not Penny, a woman in her prime.

We drove to Swindon and sat in my parents' conservatory, making a fuss of Fanny, who suddenly recognised Penny. Her tail whirred with excitement and the customary licking frenzy took place.

25 May 1999 was my fortieth birthday, and I decided to celebrate with a big party in Mallorca. Lots of friends flew over and we took over a local bar. We drank champagne and were entertained by flamenco dancers.

Two nights later, we were having a more sedate gathering on my balcony when my phone rang. It was my sister, Beverley, calling from Swindon.

'I'm sorry,' she said. 'But Fanny had to be put to sleep today.'

Fanny had taken to her bed the day before and wasn't able to move. The vet came to my parents' house and said that Fanny would never get out of the bed again. It was time. My parents weren't up to dealing with the situation so Beverley, a calm, practical primary school teacher, came to take charge.

'The vet was very kind and gentle with her,' Beverley told

me. 'Fanny didn't even notice the injection and it was all very peaceful.'

Ah, Fanny. I was so sorry I hadn't been there at the end, but my parents and sister had made the right decision. Then I remembered my command that she stay with me until my fortieth birthday. Conscientious star that she was, Fanny the Wonder Dog had fulfilled her contractual obligation. The queen of the choc drops had now departed.

Her passing made the BBC News.

Fanny was cremated. A few weeks later I collected her ashes, which I keep on a table in the hall, giving them a gentle pat each time I pass.

PART TWO
Valerie

'My sunshine doesn't come from the skies,
It comes from the love in my dog's eyes.'

Anonymous poet

CHAPTER 10

Urges in Sutton

It is said of pugs, 'They make you laugh a little louder, smile a little brighter and live a little better than before.' It's a bold claim. One that might be attached to various things, from dog breeds to nitrous oxide. In the weeks after Fanny died people asked, as people always do, 'Are you going to get another dog?' I would answer, 'Yes, eventually, when the time is right.' I mentioned to friends that pugs looked like fun, and they agreed. Apparently pugs have 'personality'. And they are undeniably camp.

Mandy my agent, together with Lisa Clark, TV producer and chum, both of whom had been on the Mallorca balcony with me when my sister had called to tell me about Fanny's demise, and who had therefore witnessed my distress, went further. They hatched a plan to present me with a pug as a surprise, thus putting a stop to my mourning and setting me on the path to happiness. It is an agent's sworn duty to keep her client happy, after all.

They turned up at my flat one Friday evening, giggling excitedly, and presented me with a medium-sized box tied with a pink ribbon. Inside was a dear little pug puppy. Three months old, fawn with a black scrunched-up nose and ears. Adorable. I lifted her out and cuddled her, overcome with surprise. I called her Maureen. Gloria the cat didn't seem keen, but that wasn't a surprise. Gloria didn't like anyone.

We drank champagne while Mandy and Lisa told me about their search for Maureen, how they had collected her from the reputable breeder the night before, the excitement of meeting outside my house and placing her in the box. I cried with gratitude and amazement. They stayed until midnight and I was left alone with my new dog. I looked at her and she looked at me. I felt . . . nothing. Not a twinge of affection or warmth. I was aghast at my lack of feeling. Maureen was mine now, my responsibility – she needed and expected my love. She looked at me with round, dark eyes full of need. I picked her up and took her to bed with me. I'd feel different in the morning, I reasoned. Her unexpected arrival was a shock, that's all. Tomorrow I'd wake up and look at her and fondness would flutter inside me and love would open up like a lotus flower until she was the centre of my life.

These things couldn't be rushed.

But in the morning I felt no different. I hadn't slept well. Maureen snored loudly. Well, she made a strange snoring sound when she was awake, but when she was asleep it was louder, like a lawnmower with a spanner stuck in its blades. Awake, the poor thing seemed to struggle to get air up her squished nasal passages, so she panted continuously, her open mouth a drooling, unfeasibly wide gash. Then there was the smell. She smelled cheese-and-biscuity, like a Welsh rarebit that had been left to rot in a ditch. I hesitate to pile on the criticism, but she also shed hair. She only had to twitch and cascades of it fell around her like pungent beige blossom. I gave her a bath and a brush, but the smell and the moulting remained. My friends phoned to see how the bonding process was going and I did my best to sound enthusiastic, but they sensed my lack of sincerity.

By Monday morning, I still wasn't feeling attached. The same couldn't be said for Maureen. She was besotted with me. She stared at me adoringly, followed my every move and accompanied me to the toilet, upstairs, downstairs, even from one side of the room to the other. She wanted to be beside me, on me, in me. When I took a shower, she pressed her face against the glass screen. When I passed a motion, it was with her staring up between my knees. After three days of this, I had to admit defeat. I thought I was a dog lover but I didn't feel love for this particular dog. I felt only irritation and intense dislike. I felt wretched, and agonised for several hours before I phoned Mandy and began a rather excruciating conversation.

'I'm so sorry. I can't spend the next fifteen years with this dog. I have to be honest. Please can you come and take her away? Now?'

Maureen was quickly removed from my life. I felt terribly sad for Maureen and about my own failure to like her, let alone love her. The worst thing was, she was returned to the breeder and remained there for quite a while. We kept checking to see if a home had been found for her, and it hadn't. Months passed. The thought of poor, dejected Maureen sitting there unwanted was too much. I was on the point of asking the breeder if I could have her back when I heard that an elderly widow had taken her at last. The perfect home. Maureen wouldn't be lonely any more, and neither would the widow.

There is no photographic record of Maureen, which is for the best. You must create your own image of her, which will depend, I dare say, on where you stand on pugs. Imagine huge, round, black eyes, like molasses, set unfeasibly wide so they're almost on the side of the head, like a seagull's eyes. A mouth – let's call it a gash – like the Joker's grin, stretching from ear to ear. Ears like burnt beetroot crisps perched atop a brainless head. I'll stop. I've said too much.

The moral of this sad story is that buying a dog for someone is risky. I believe you have to choose your own. Higher forces will guide you to the correct dog. We mess with the natural order of things at our peril.

Living alone with Gloria was, unsurprisingly, not a pleasant experience. Her rare displays of affection always ended in tears. Mine. If she decided to come and sit on my lap, five minutes of purring and stroking would be followed by a sudden turn of mood. Her tail would swish, her eyes narrow, and she would sink her teeth into any available flesh – hand or face, she wasn't fussy. What her problem was, I never knew. She was a tortoise-shell – they're known to be hot-tempered or, if we're being kind, high-spirited. There are a number of myths associated with cats of this colouring. In some cultures they're thought to bring good luck and are referred to as the money cat. If you dream of a tortoiseshell cat, you'll be lucky in love. Some say they have psychic abilities and can see into the future. A Khymer legend in South East Asia has it that the first tortoiseshell was created from the menstrual blood of a goddess born of a lotus flower. Be that as it may, Gloria was hard work to live with and most of the time we kept a wary distance from each other. That distance was extended permanently a few years later when I took her to my parents one weekend and left her there. She spent the rest of her days sitting on the kitchen windowsill glowering at the world with what passes for contentment when you're Beelzebub.

Only six months after Fanny died, and four months after my hellish weekend with the unfortunate Maureen, the familiar, gnawing need to get a puppy came over me. It reached a peak on 5 November 1999. I was filming a Daz advert in a shopping centre in Sutton. As you do. 'New Daz tablets. Prepare to be dazzled!'

A luxury Winnebago had been provided for my dressing room, and we were discreetly located in the corner of the car park, away from the prying eyes of the curious public. My long-suffering assistant Bec (always referred to as 'Bertha the lesbian' for light entertainment purposes) had given birth to her son, Alfie, a few months previously, and was spending a lot of time in the toilet noisily expressing milk using an electric breast pump. It was this, I think, that brought on my own maternal desires.

'When you've finished in there, Bertha,' I called through the door, 'could you see if there's a pet shop in Sutton? I need a puppy. Today!'

One of the less pleasant side-effects of showbiz success is that stars can make unreasonable demands of their staff, which are never challenged. No doubt Bertha rolled her eyes as she tidied herself up in the bathroom, but she emerged with a compliant smile and went in search of a pet shop. She'd never failed me before. Bertha returned half an hour later to say she had located a litter of puppies for sale. I was elated and felt my own nipples twinge with excitement.

'What sort?' I asked.

'Cocker spaniels,' she answered.

'But that's no good! I want a whippety crossbreed!' I cried in dismay.

'Proper' dog breeds didn't interest me and spaniels, lovely as they are, always look so sad and needy, even when they're happy. Then there's their tendency to flaky skin and psoriasis. There's enough sweeping up goes on in my house due to my digestive biscuit habit. No. I think I had some vague notion about reincarnation in my mind. Fanny was out there somewhere, reborn, and I had to find out where she was.

It so happened that my driver for the day, Dave (they are invariably called Dave), was stretching his legs outside the Winnebago and heard my plaintive words. He knocked on the door.

'Apologies. Couldn't help but overhear your conversation. . . My mate mentioned that his girlfriend's dog, a lovely whippet called Blue, has some puppies. Might they be of interest? I could give him a ring and see if they're still looking for homes.'

I knew at once, before he had finished speaking, that Dave would lead me to my next dog. I love it when fate steps in and you're led to your destiny, as if by the subtle manipulations of a god. It seemed 'right'. Resistance was futile.

Once we had finished filming, Dave drove us to a housing estate in Clapham. Blue's owner wouldn't be home until seven, so we had a few anxious hours to wait. Even though I was in full make-up and wearing a two-tone purple suit with a large diamante brooch on the lapel, we decided to go to a pub, where my order of a snowball with vodka – 'and don't forget the cherry on a stick' – aroused aggressive curiosity in some of the locals. Dave was suddenly promoted to minder duties, until Bertha decided we should retreat to the Mercedes and wait there. I was as anxious as an expectant father until Dave recognised a blonde woman with a pushchair and a toddler entering the flats.

'That's her,' he said.

Inside the flat two adorable puppies flung themselves at me while Blue, their mother, looked on proudly. Both were bitches, black with a token white dash on their chests, but quite different. One was slightly larger, with a smooth coat and floppy ears. The smaller one had longer, wiry fur and big, upright, bat-like ears. I could have taken either, or both, but after I lifted each one up and looked into their eyes and pressed their forehead to mine (I'm not sure why. I probably thought I was Mystic Meg), I chose the larger pup. She had a similar vibe to Fanny, I was sure of it. It was the second coming, right there in Clapham.

With my new dog tucked under my arm, I had a chat with the owner. Blue was a special dog, she told me, very loving and affectionate. She had chosen her mate carefully – a handsome local pit bull terrier who could understand over thirty commands. There had been five puppies in the litter and the three boys had already gone. They were seven weeks old. The remaining puppy was jumping up, trying to get at her sister, and I felt awful separating them. But an idea was forming in my mind.

'I take it you'd like to find a home for the last one?' I asked.

The owner nodded. I took her number and said I'd call if I could help. I thanked her and carried my new dog down to the Mercedes, wrapped in a towel. She pressed her head against me, shaking and whimpering with worry. It was bonfire night, and as we drove past Clapham Common we found ourselves in the midst of a huge, cacophonous firework display. The puppy was sick with fear. Warm, half-digested Pedigree Chum dripped down my suit, which Bertha did her best to clean.

But we were soon home in Camden, where my sister Frankie was waiting to greet us. After much cooing and fussing we put the puppy on the floor on some newspaper to see if she needed a wee. She didn't. Instead she scampered across the kitchen to a small Moroccan rug and sat down for a good scratch. She peered at us as we made reassuring noises at her and offered her water, biscuits and toys, which she declined. However much we tried to entice her, she wouldn't move from the rug or even stand up. She was in shock, understandably, after being removed from her mother and sister and the only home she had ever known.

I got down on the floor, stroking her, telling her that everything would be fine and I'd look after her. She was still trembling, and she kept closing her eyes for a few seconds then opening them, as if hoping to find she was back in Clapham with Blue. I scratched her under the chin and stroked her. I whispered in her ear as I used to with Fanny, who always found it comforting. But it didn't seem to have a calming effect on this little girl at all.

As I pulled away, I saw something moving inside her ear. I called my sister to come and have a look. All around the puppy's ears and eyes were minuscule mites. We looked along her back and there were more, bigger critters. Not just one or two, but hundreds – fleas, bugs or mites, I had no idea what they were, but the poor dog was alive with them. Underneath her fur, her skin was speckled with blood and angry-looking rashes.

'Poor thing!' said my sister. 'They must be driving her insane.'

The puppy's pained expression and shakes were no doubt partly due to the fright of being separated from her mother, and the noisy fireworks, but also the excruciating discomfort of having every inch of her skin infested with parasites. We decided it couldn't wait until morning, found a twenty-four-hour vet and drove straight there.

The treatment – a solution absorbed through the skin, ear drops and a painkiller – was immediately effective. The critters dropped off in their droves. By the time we got her home again, she was a different puppy. Free from the torture of being eaten alive, she looked calm and happy. She even wagged her tail for the first time and began to respond to us and tentatively explore her surroundings. Our immediate assessment was that she was a gentle, kind soul. She didn't display the energy and adventurous spirit that Fanny had been infused with, but a wiser, calmer, more contemplative personality.

But it was early days. She hadn't come out of her shell yet.

'So what are you going to call her?' asked my sister when the puppy finally dozed off on my lap.

I felt that a sophisticated name would suit this dog. 'She has the air of a posh secretary about her,' I said. 'Something like Annabelle?'

Frankie shook her head. 'She's nothing like a posh secretary.

Where on earth do you get that from? Why don't you call her Daz, after the advert?'

I considered this a serious contender, but wondered if the novelty might wear off after a while. 'If only I'd been advertising Omo . . .'.

Generally, I prefer 'human' names for animals, but there are exceptions. I've known two Jack Russells delightfully called Taxi and Rocket. But could I really call 'Daz!' in the park in a loud voice? For all I knew, it was code for some sort of drug, like Spice or Ice. . .

'Crystal?' I wondered. No. Crystal meth.

A while later, the right name suddenly occurred to me. 'Her name is Valerie,' I said.

'Yes,' agreed my sister. 'Valerie is the correct name.'

Puppy christened, it was time for bed. I decided, after nineteen years with Fanny sleeping in my bed, that I would do things differently this time. I wanted Valerie to get used to sleeping in a basket in my bedroom – close to me, but not quite as close as Fanny.

Unlike Fanny, Valerie didn't express any dissatisfaction with her sleeping arrangements. Tired and emotional, we both fell asleep quickly and slept soundly until morning.

CHAPTER 11

Valerie Has No Talent

I couldn't get the thought of the other puppy I had left behind in Clapham out of my mind. No doubt she was covered in the same mites as Valerie, and I wanted her to be rescued as soon as possible. It would be wonderful if Valerie could have contact with her sibling, too. . . When I met them and chose Valerie, I had a bit of a psychic flash: a vision of a friend of mine with the smaller pup. Who knows why this image popped into my head? But I don't like to ignore these things when they happen. I just had to alert my friend to this exciting news. He lived nearby, worked in the theatre in the evenings, and had a large garden. Best of all, he was suggestible. I phoned him to tell him all about Valerie.

'She has a sister. The loveliest little dog. I don't know why, but I think you should have her.'

'Me? Get a puppy?' my friend said doubtfully.

'Well, yes. She needs to be rescued and she's perfect for you. You'll love her.'

'I don't know. . .'.

'Well, I do. You're having her. Get used to the idea.'

'I'll think about it.'

'Go and see her. If you don't like her, then don't take her. But you will.'

'Um. . .'.

"I know I'm right about this. I'm never wrong.' I'd decided a firm hand was called for. 'Go today. Go now.'

So he did. And I was right. He named Valerie's sister Queen Latifah. A few weeks later, after both puppies had had their injections, they were reunited. It was like a scene from *Born Free*. They rushed to greet each other, kissing, wrestling, yelping with excitement as we humans glowed with contagious joy. After that we'd meet in Regent's Park every week or so. The puppies would spot each other in the distance and charge towards another euphoric encounter. It was like an episode of *Long Lost Family*, but with better teeth.

As she settled in, Valerie's calm but shy nature emerged. She was a circumspect dog, given to quiet, thoughtful moments. She looked a bit like an athletic mini-Labrador. Her coat was sleek and as glossy as wet paint. She liked to sit in the sunshine, where her fur sometimes had an almost purple hue to it – a genetic result, I supposed, of her mother's blue colouring and whatever else had gone into the mix. Her expressive, intelligent eyes were the colour of vintage brandy and there was an aura of kindness about her.

She learned things very quickly and seemed to have a strong moral code. Having been told not to get on my bed at night, she never attempted it again. Even when I was upset, when I wanted the comfort of her lying next to me and called her and patted the mattress temptingly, she wouldn't respond. She'd look vaguely horrified that I was considering breaking the rules. If I lifted her onto the bed she would jump straight off then glance back at me, outraged, as if I had suggested a threesome with a Tory MP.

I rather grandly decided that I was too famous to go on public transport myself (it was a phase. . .) so I asked friends to spend a few hours taking Valerie on tube, bus and train outings to acclimatise her to the sights and sounds of urban life. I stayed at home, shielding myself from the horrors of interacting with the public. Valerie enjoyed life rather passively and didn't go into protective mode – barking and that sort of carry-on – unless pressed. Any unusual bumps in the night and she would sit up, wide-eyed, possibly offer a quiet 'oof!' to alert me, but she would not investigate herself.

She was very specific about the dogs she liked to play with. There wasn't a particular 'type'; I presume it was to do with personality or pheromones. If a dog met her exacting criteria, she would chase and wrestle endlessly. If not, she would turn away disdainfully or, if that didn't discourage attempts at intimacy, she would jut her head forward and curl her lip, baring her lovely white teeth. A proper scrap was very rare for Valerie: any fights were over in seconds – just a quick flash of pit bull temper would see any aggressor off. I barely had time to put my best Pat Butcher voice on and say, 'Leave it, Val, it's not worth it.'

But Valerie's top-of-the-range excitement was reserved for Queen Latifah. Even if she had seen her the day before, their mutual jubilation knew no bounds.

Given my fancy that my new dog might be Fanny the Wonder

Dog reincarnated, I thought the best way to confirm my suspicion was to take her on stage with me at the earliest opportunity. I was booked to perform a late-night gig at a Butlin's 'adult weekend' event near Lowestoft. (It paid well. What can I say?) I decided I would test her out there. It was a rowdy crowd, and I suspected they had keenly accepted the 'all you can drink' offering. Halfway through my set, Bertha handed me Valerie from the wings and I carried her on stage to a response of noisy bays and whistles.

It did not go well. Under those circumstances Fanny, in her prime, would have stared back at the hecklers and won them over. Valerie shrank in my arms and shook like a leaf, refusing to even look at the audience. I decided to abort.

When I passed her back to Bertha in the safety of the wings, the crowd's noisy applause just about finished her off. Valerie wasn't a born performer. She didn't care to be in the spotlight and, lovely as she was, there was no sign that she was Fanny Mark II. The Butlin's experience put her off for life. On future tours, if she ever wandered on stage during the sound check, a haunted look appeared in her eyes and she would hotfoot it to the safety of the darkened wings. In my heartless pursuit of cheap laughs I would introduce her thus: 'This is Valerie. She has no talent. She is the Prince Andrew of the dog world.'

A few weeks after Valerie's arrival I started rehearsals for my first ever panto season, which was *Cinderella* at the Theatre Royal in Brighton. Following my instructions to the letter, she would sit attentively by the rehearsal room wall and watch bemused as I went through my scenes and 'sang' my monotone version of M

People's 'Search for the Hero' surrounded by children dressed as squirrels, badgers and foxes. Once the panto was up and running she rested in my dressing room during performances, listening to the show on the tannoy and casting her eyes over me when I popped in for my many costume changes. Since there were two shows a day, it didn't take her long to 'learn' the show. The finale music was her cue for the glazed expression to leave her face, for her to stand up and stretch, sure in the knowledge that the nonsense was over and an outing to the Brighton sea front imminent.

Talking of nonsense, at this time I was attempting an affair with Robin, a concert pianist I met at a party, who had two lovely dogs, a Jack Russell and a Staffie. I met him after one of his concerts. The first thing he said to me was, 'Do you know Bach's *Organ Works*?'

I said, 'Yes, so does mine.'

There was an immediate attraction between us. But we couldn't do anything about it because he had a boyfriend who was ginger and therefore very, very sensitive. There was a six-month period of unrequited passion – every time we bumped into each other we were dripping and bulging with anticipation. It was unhealthy. To cut a long story medium-length, he dumped the ginger minger, phoned me up and said he was on his way round to my place.

I was so excited. I rushed round the house, lit some scented candles and put the champagne on ice. I had a quick prostitute's wash then lubed up every available orifice. Because you just don't know on a first date, do you? Then the doorbell went and there he was, carrying a holdall. I said, 'Come in.' He said, 'Before we start, let's have a chat about what I like in the bedroom.'

I thought, well, it's a funny time to discuss my soft furnishings. He said, 'No. In my holdall I have a length of rope, some clothes pegs and a sink plunger. How do you feel about a little light S&M?'

I said, 'Hang on, there's a branch in the high street. They do a very good low-calorie salad.'

He said, 'No, that's M&S. I'm talking S&M. I'd like to tie you up and spank you with a flip-flop.'

I thought, well, the dog won't like that.

We embarked on this S&M nonsense. It's such a palaver. He told me I'd have to have a 'safe' word. I chose 'Chatham'. (Guaranteed to cause the most urgent erection to wither on the vine. What a shithole.) The relationship limped on for a while, but there was no spontaneity. If we were feeling frisky, Robin had to go downstairs and fetch his holdall. Then he had to lay out the rope, the gag, the grease gun. Sometimes by the time he'd finished I'd sent half a dozen emails and done a phone interview with Three Counties Radio. Why we couldn't just have sex over the bean bag with the Bee Gees playing like everyone else, I don't know.

I was overusing my safe word. He'd say, 'Good morning', I'd say, 'Chatham'. He'd say, 'Would you like a cup of tea?', I'd say, 'Chatham'.

He was rather keener on the arrangement than I was, and seemed to be under the impression that stepping out with me was akin to winning the lottery. Just like Fanny, Valerie's

I was one of a litter of three. Here I am with my sisters, Beverley and Frances on holiday in Cornwall with our newly acquired dachshund puppy Monty.

Nick and I passed the time dressing up and creating elaborate tableaux. The symbolism of this one is lost in the mists of time.

Left: My sister Frankie came to tea with her daughters in my tiny flat in Kidbrooke.

On a break from the Edinburgh Festival Fanny and I would take the air in the sand dunes.

My dressing room at the Hackney Empire. I appear to be enjoying a can of lager.

Left: For the cover of my not-quite-a-hit-single I channelled my inner Marlon Brando.

Below: An early attempt at light entertainment on the telly box. Mike Smith's suit was a lot cheaper than mine.

Above: Camping in Australia with the Lovely Russell who would open his eyes only when told to.

Right: With Christopher in the days when wire coat hangers were tolerated.

Right: When Christopher took to our bed Fanny went with him.

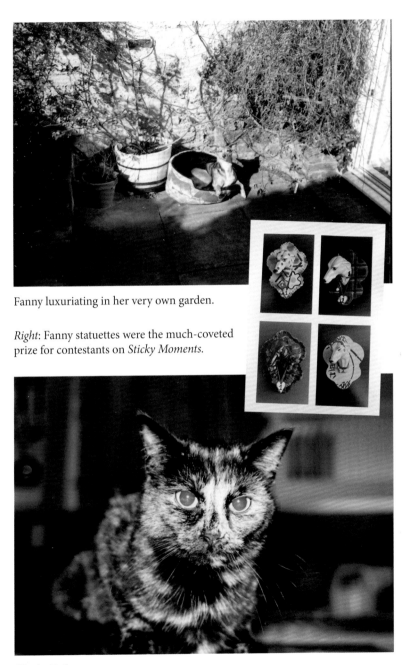

Fanny luxuriating in her very own garden.

Right: Fanny statuettes were the much-coveted prize for contestants on *Sticky Moments*.

Gloria. Evil.

Visiting Steven on the Broderip Ward, Middlesex Hospital.

Valerie doing her best to satisfy my showbiz whims, although being on stage was not for her.

Left: With Drew Jaymson-Neal back stage in Taboo. Make-up was involved.

Below: Valerie (right) with her sister Latifah in the Lake District. A cushion might have been nice.

Valerie and me going for a casual stroll through Camden.

assessment of my gentlemen callers was always swift and accurate. She didn't like Robin. Tellingly, she yawned whenever he entered the room. Soon I was doing the same. My attention span with men has always been an issue. I put him off coming to Brighton to see me, saying that my schedule was so full-on I wouldn't be much fun. But it was his birthday and he turned up anyway. I feigned delight. Valerie's yawn was so wide, I feared she might dislocate her jaw. While I did my matinee one day, he went for a stroll around the Lanes. He returned in a state of high excitement. 'I've just seen the birthday present you can buy me!'

It was a vintage gold Rolex.

Bold.

My sister Frankie was working as my dresser. While I was on stage that evening, she and Robin chatted in my dressing room. He told her all about his dilapidated home in Derby and his plans for a swanky barn conversion in the garden. 'Julian doesn't know yet, but he's going to be paying for it,' he told her with a wink.

She told me. I told him it was over.

He didn't take it well and in the end he called me frigid; That couldn't be further from the truth. If I've had enough to drink, I've been known to find traffic cones attractive. Especially those fluorescent ones. I've had my way with one or two of them.

Robin now lives in Hull with someone he met on the website slaveboy.com. I wish them every happiness.

On a roll, I decided it would make sense to find another dysfunctional boyfriend. Out of the frying pan, into the furnace. Who doesn't love a bad boy?

This time I chose a rugged lager drinker with a shaved head. Ideal. All that belchy sex and his moody hangovers must have convinced me he was 'the one', because when he became homeless soon after I met him, I invited him to move in with me. Valerie looked on in horror, although she benefited in a roundabout way – when the dinners I made for him, which he never came home to eat, ended up on her plate. If he made it home at all it was in the small hours, stumbling and smelling of vomit and tripping over the dog as she slept. When I questioned him about the love bites on his neck, his answer – 'There's nothing there' – didn't convince me.

I came to my senses and told him to move out. I thought he might say, 'I'm not here,' but to give him his due, he packed his bags – and bottles – and left. Valerie and I sighed with relief. I was obviously at a stage in my life where I was seeking a relationship. I just hadn't found the right person. The drama of dating the mad, sad or bad was to go on for a while before I found a suitable match. Finding the right man is harder than finding the right dog, it seems.

Talking of which, the next spring Valerie came into season. I was so worried that history would repeat itself and that ginormous, unwanted puppies would soon be fired at me that I took Valerie to the vet and asked if there was anything he could give her to prevent her coming into season. A visit to the vet is more or less guaranteed to bring on a panic attack. I'm anxious before I get there, as is the dog – by process of osmosis, no doubt. I like to be in and out quickly, before my heart rate gets out of control and sweat soaks through my shirt. But my vet liked to give clients their money's-worth, and wasn't to be rushed. He enjoyed the sound of his own voice and over the years I had grown to fear his long digressions. I took Gloria in once, I forget why, and his mini-lecture culminated in a drawing of a cat's bottom, which he asked if I'd like to keep.

No doubt he told me about the dangers and possible side-effects of the injection he was administering to Valerie but, to my great regret, I didn't listen. I just wanted the inconvenience of her season to stop, and to get out of there. That weekend I went to see my parents, where Valerie slept in the kitchen. She had a severe haemorrhage overnight – the kitchen looked like an abattoir the next morning. We rushed Valerie to a local vet, where she had to have a hysterectomy. Her recovery was slow and painful and I blamed myself entirely – the hot flush of guilt creeps over me even now as I write of this sorry incident. I should have properly weighed up the dangers of the injection and thought of her well-being rather than my own convenience. I had messed with nature and Valerie had paid the price. But she didn't know I was the instigator of her suffering. She gazed at me with unjustified adoration, and I wept and loved her all the more. Luckily for me, dogs don't do blame or resentment – fairly useless feelings best left to the unhappily married.

With the pink scar on her tummy an emblem of my failing as her guardian, we began rehearsals for the Boy George musical *Taboo*. I was to take over the role of the outrageously attired Leigh Bowery from George at the Venue (now called the Leicester Square Theatre). My head was shaved for the part, which Valerie didn't seem to notice, but others did. For the first time in my life I had the novelty of looking threatening. I rather enjoyed pedestrians swerving to avoid me on the street, lest I pull out a knife and slash them.

It was a wonderful show. Everyone got on very well. I particularly relished my opening scene, in which I emerged from a toilet cubicle with a green face with orange polka dots, in a matching suit, and sang:

> *I've had a man or two,*
> *In fact, I've had a few*
> *In dark and dingy places. . .*[6]

The Venue was a small theatre and, with a fairly large cast, backstage was crowded. There were only two small dressing rooms, quaintly designated 'Boys' and 'Girls', where we sat in rows along two counters, each performer allowed their own body width to display and apply their make-up – of which there was heaps, this being a musical set in 1980s clubland. Valerie had a space to curl up under the counter by my feet.

To my right sat Dan Carter, a member of the ensemble who understudied Steve Strange's and Marilyn's parts, and with whom I had what the young people call 'banter'. He was that rare thing in musical theatre: a heterosexual man. I would chastise him for infringing on my space, make disparaging remarks about his nerdy computer-savvy ways, about his domestic arrangements (he lived with his parents in Bexleyheath and had a golden Labrador called Max), and quiz him about the colour of their sofa (beige) and his busy love life. Despite the lack of counter space, and to give Dan something to complain about, I brought in a large silver-framed photo of Valerie taken on a recent holiday to the Lake District, in which she sat statuesquely in a bucolic landscape of green hills.

Dan scoffed. 'You don't need a photo of her, surely? If you need to see what she looks like, just open your legs.'

'How dare you. I did not come here to be insulted by a chorus boy from Bexleyheath.'

'Where do you normally go?'

A few days later, during the interval I glanced at the portrait of Valerie and let out a cry of horror. The photo had been digitally altered somehow so it just showed green hills – Valerie had gone! I was suitably outraged. Dan denied all knowledge, but of course he was the culprit.

The next day Valerie was back in the frame, wearing a Scottish hat and playing bagpipes.

There were other shenanigans, of course. I came off stage after one scene to see an actor dressed in full mufti, legs splayed, dress hitched up to his waist, using his hands to hold his bum cheeks apart while another actor aimed M&Ms at his arsehole. Practice made perfect.

Two-show days meant a rather long day in the theatre for Valerie, so if possible I left her at home and arranged for a dog walker. My old school friend Nick had a break between shifts at the pub and a spare key, so sometimes he obliged. This arrangement came to an end after a neighbour told me she'd come across Valerie standing in the park the previous afternoon, Nick lying next to her, passed out with his head in a puddle. The drink had got a firm grip on Nick, and he was increasingly bleary-eyed and bloated when I saw him, although if I raised the subject he'd be defensive and ask what harm a drink or two after work could do. More tellingly, when I opened the front door to greet him, Valerie would back away with a look of horror on her face, and there would be a suspicious clinking of bottles from his bag as he placed it on the floor.

With my dog-sitter out of action, I went back to bringing Valerie to the theatre with me again whenever possible. The modest wages I earned for *Taboo* helped me overcome my disdain for public transport. Valerie and I travelled to work and home again on the number 29 bus, which dropped me conveniently at the top of Tottenham Court Road. The bus home was busy at weekends, full of revellers on their way to sample the joys of Camden's throbbing nightlife. One Friday evening I squeezed into a window seat, hat pulled down over my face to avoid unwanted attention, with Valerie on the floor between my legs. I didn't turn to look, but in the window I saw the reflection of the man who sat next to me. He was rough, and not in a good way. Big, forty-ish, reeking of alcohol, and panting and wheezing as if he'd had to run to catch the bus. A quick glance told me his knuckles were freshly grazed. Who knows what his story was? I thought.

I felt the lead pull as Valerie changed position. I thought I'd better check on her, so I moved my legs to one side and looked down. She was licking the rough man's boots. Then I realised what was so tasty: blood. Red and jelly-ish. Maybe it was ketchup? No. It was blood. And flesh. The man sitting next to me had clearly just been involved in a fracas. I pulled the lead tighter to stop Valerie, but she was enjoying her unexpected snack and pulled back. The man got off the bus before me, so I didn't have to risk revealing my identity to a stranger with a suspected tendency for GBH. Safely home ten minutes later, I contemplated alerting the police, but decided that the fact that my dog had licked the boots of a burly man on the 29 bus might not be of much interest to them.

We didn't know it at the time, but there was another burly, boot-wearing alpha male waiting in the wings for Valerie. It never rains but it pours.

CHAPTER 12

Valerie Takes Charge

Celebrity Dog School was a BBC1 series in which celebs and their dogs worked together with dog trainers in a bid to see who had the best-trained pooch. As the tantalising press release put it: 'Will Johnny Vaughan's bulldog Harvey prove to be more popular than Michelle Ryan's Labrador pup, Buddy? Ronnie Corbett certainly fancies his chances with his two miniature Schnauzer puppies, Rag and Muffin, but faces stiff competition from Julian Clary's mongrel, Valerie.'[7]

Valerie was naturally well behaved so, apart from teaching her to sit and fetch a stick, I hadn't troubled with much formal training. In fact, it has to be said, after a few years with the stone-deaf Fanny, I had got out of the habit of talking to my dog much. But the sight of the other celebs and their pure-breed mutts – Dora Bryan and her Tibetan terrier Georgie and Linda Barker's dachshund puppy Tiger Lily – clearly brought out my dormant competitive streak.

Never one to shy away from rejigging an old line, I told the press: 'Valerie is the most intelligent and attractive dog taking part in the competition. She's the Germaine Greer of the dog world and if she doesn't win I'll put her to sleep.' Viewers voted by telephone for their favourite dog throughout the series, which was to raise money for Children In Need.

We might think professional dog trainers are nice, cuddly types who aren't too fussed about personal freshness, and in general that might be true. But it was our misfortune to be paired with an army sergeant major whose job was to train military dogs in combat situations to sniff out cadavers. To say he was no-nonsense is a bit like describing Rose West as a party girl.

'I'm a military man and failure is not an option,' he told me sternly. 'Valerie's a bit standoffish.'

Well, good for her, I thought. There was a lot of barking and it wasn't from Valerie. This had comic potential, of course, and I wasn't above playing up for the cameras – my Melvyn Hayes to his Windsor Davies. When teaching Valerie to walk to heel, he complained that I was mincing. I enjoyed his discomfort when I told him he had lovely eyes. Goat's eyes.

'You'll make someone a lovely yoghurt one day,' I simpered.

But it was Valerie I felt protective of. She was a shy, gentle dog. She didn't like his shouty ways and I objected when he called her 'timid'. She was serene, I explained – not an asset of much use on the battlefield, perhaps. Valerie hated raised voices. I had to turn *EastEnders* off when the Mitchells were going at each other.

Despite all this, I grudgingly had to admit that the sergeant major knew his stuff. Valerie knew how to come and sit, but he taught her to lie down and roll over (always useful). Then to stay, wait, retrieve and master an obstacle course (less useful, frankly).

But along with her sensitive nature Valerie was highly intelligent and she tuned into the sergeant major's wavelength and did what was required, daintily and in her own style. She rather liked him, I observed, so I decided to be kinder to him myself.

'If all this works, I shall grow a moustache in your honour,' I told him. I was suitably proud when Valerie won first place in the final and was presented with a large silver cup (well, silver *coloured*, you understand). I never did grow a moustache, though.

I had reason to be grateful to *Celebrity Dog School* some months later, as it turned out. I was visiting Auntie Tess in Brentford. Just as we got out of my car Valerie spotted a squirrel on the other side of the road and gave chase, pulling the lead from my hand. Cars swerved to avoid her while I suffered flashbacks of Fanny's accident in Newcastle. Valerie made it to the other side of the road, the squirrel disappeared and she was stranded there, two lanes of busy traffic thundering between us. She looked over to me and was about to dive across the road when I remembered our training.

'No! Valerie, wait! Sit. WAIT!'

And she did. She sat calmly on the roadside until I, heart in mouth, was able to mince across and rescue her. God bless the sergeant major. I won't hear a word against him.

While all this was going on, auditions continued for the position of my boyfriend. I was very thorough. I took to going on holiday with some rather chic friends who knew how to have a good time. Ivan and Jasper rented a villa in St Tropez for several summers, and I worked my way through all the local contenders. It was an admirably brisk process. Relationships consisted of just

four words: 'You'll do', 'Slower' and 'Taxi'. After I'd checked out
every available man and had my fill of crusty French sticks at
that location, we moved on to Ibiza. And it was there, at a party
on a yacht in 2002, that I encountered the man who was to share
my life and my dogs and who I would marry fourteen years later.

Not that I knew this exciting fact at the time. Or maybe, on
some level I did. My stage act, for all its dedication to triviality,
has always been where I subconsciously work through my real-
life issues, albeit in a comedic, fantastical form. My fervent desire
to be swept off my feet in a romantic seaside setting in my private
life was certainly reflected in my on-stage musings:

> I was on Bondi Beach and I went in for a dip. But little did I
> know that beneath the waves was the Sydney Gay Sub-Aqua
> Club. The next thing I knew, my Speedos were off and I'd
> been sucked under.
>
> Well, I put up a bit of a struggle. But suddenly I was swept
> up into the arms of a lifeguard and carried back to dry land.
> He said his name was Rolf.

It's like positive affirmations, I think: if you repeat something
often enough – even, or perhaps especially, on stage – it will
eventually become a reality.

So, there he was on the yacht. I'll call him Rolf. He had dark
hair and slim hips, so I naturally assumed he was a Spanish
waiter and handed him my empty champagne glass, vaguely
wondering if I might lure him into the broom cupboard on the
poop deck later if the party got messy. In fact, he was English

and an acquaintance of Ivan, who had a hunch that we might get on. Which we did. He was northern, if you please. I've dated a few northerners in my time – nice, sturdy people who don't feel the cold so you don't need to bother about the central heating. And despite my southern preconceptions they do, in fact, know how to use cutlery and can occasionally be persuaded to take a shower. His accent was a worry, but I knew I could afford to pay for elocution lessons should the relationship be a goer and conversation be deemed necessary.

I'm going to stick with calling him Rolf here, to protect the innocent. Rolf tells me he has no desire to have his private life written about for the entertainment of the general public. This is quite annoying, and something I wish he'd made clear when I met him on the yacht, but I'd better comply in the interests of marital harmony. Personally I can't think of anything nicer than documenting every twinge of my sphincter for all and sundry, but then I've always had a tendency to overshare. Well, it wouldn't do if we were all the same. We must struggle on with Rolf as a shadowy presence – which, between you and me, is art imitating life anyway.

So, I met Rolf and registered that there was something rather acceptable there. We spent several days and evenings together (unusually, we kept ourselves nice). But Rolf's job was running Ministry of Sound at Pacha nightclub so, while he had a flat in London, he was living and working in Ibiza. A short hop from Mallorca, I realised, so I lured him to my apartment in Puerto Andratx at the next available opportunity. Then, at the end of the season, he returned to London and our relationship got tentatively under way. More importantly, he got to meet Valerie. This test he passed with flying colours. They adored each other, just as I'd hoped. So intense was their love for each other, in fact, that I was sometimes excluded. They would occupy the sofa, snuggling and necking like teenagers, while I was relegated to the armchair on the other side of the lounge. Be careful what you wish for.

Sometimes, to fully realise how important something is to you, it has to be taken from your grasp first – like the closure of public toilets during a lockdown. Rolf – young, handsome, clever, clean-living, Valerie's heart-throb – was husband material if ever there was. His only vice was chocolate and his only fault was being faultless. This made arguing an uneven activity.

'You're drunk! You're self-centred! You're vain!'

How was I to respond? 'You're . . . thin!'

Not a bona fide insult, I hasten to add, in case someone with a 28-inch waist happens to be perusing this book.

Rolf's main asset was that he never bored me – which was unheard of in a suitor. But before I fully committed and snapped him up, he got another job with a creative agency and was offered the apparently unmissable opportunity to go and work in Los Angeles. This is the downside of talented, ambitious partners; they will insist on having their own lives and it isn't always convenient. What was I to do? What was Valerie to do? We waved him off and he moved into a loft apartment in LA and drove a flashy car around Venice Beach.

I visited, but things didn't go well. As I walked across the airport terminal to meet him, my front tooth fell out. Not only was I disfigured, but we also had to spend three days sorting out dentistry that cost as much as a luxury holiday in the Caribbean. I've never been that enamoured with America. I'd taken my act to New York a couple of times, but buggery jokes didn't seem to be their thing and the audiences liked to shout a lot. Frankly, if I want to be talked over and ignored and made to feel like shit, I can be a guest on *Loose Women*. It must be difficult for Americans, I always think, trying to express yourself with such a limited vocabulary.

Rolf was gone, and I missed him. I'm not the needy sort and I knew I would manage, but I was concerned about Valerie. Her only consolation was the occasional reunion with her sister Queen Latifah, but despite this she seemed in a constant state of wistfulness. I decided it was my duty as a dog owner to do everything in my power to get Rolf back to the mother country as soon as possible.

Home alone, I no longer felt like going out on the town and sniffing about for gentlemen callers, so I bought a holiday flat in Brighton so I could spend my days off enjoying a blow on the front. I met a man in Brighton who wanted to lie on the floor and lick my naked feet. This I consented to, although it did nothing for me and was a bit distracting when I was on the phone to my mother. Valerie moved as far away from him as possible, but as he was on her level, she found him hard to ignore. She looked away from him – with his hungry, waggling tongue – up to me, her eyes pleading, so I told him it had been lovely but he'd better go now.

With domestic bliss slipping from my grasp, I thought I'd better distract myself with work. As luck would have it, my agent called with an offer that sounded interesting. Would I like to take part in the second series of *Strictly Come Dancing*? Why not? I thought. My sister Frankie was a professional dancer, and I was sure dancing was in my blood. It would be camp and it would distract me from my unwanted isolation. My pro dance partner was Erin Boag, a New Zealander. The Kiwi accent mixes up vowel sounds, so it was little wonder I took a while to understand her instructions.

'Loft fut to the rit,' she said. I'd been similarly confused during a gig in Auckland once, when a punter I had on stage told me he worked for a charity called Grin Piss.

It turned out Erin wanted me to move my left foot to the right. But once I had tuned into her funny ways and she into mine we got along splendidly, fully embracing our teacher/pupil roles.

'We're not going home until you git it rit,' Erin said firmly. 'It's up to you if that takes tin minutes or three hoars.'

'I don't like your tone,' I replied. 'I am a major celebrity, in case you've forgotten.'

'Tough,' said Erin. 'They din't call me Miss Whiplish for nothing.'

'My agent shall hear of this.'

'From the tip,' said Erin, marching to the centre of the dance floor, flicking her hair back determinedly.

'Valerie!' I called. 'Bite Erin, please. Good dog. Bite the nasty dancer woman. . .'.

But Valerie didn't move, just rested her head wearily on her paws.

We had ten weeks of dancing ahead of us, as things worked out. Valerie became accustomed to watching me attempt various ballroom and Latin dances every day, and it was only when the body language expert on *It Takes Two* commented on it that I realised Erin and I were communicating through Valerie, negotiating – via her passive presence – the boundaries and commitment of our partnership.

'Valerie wants to go home,' I would say.

'Valerie wants you to git it rit,' Erin would reply.

It slowly dawned on me that I wasn't a naturally gifted dancer and that maybe I had been cast as the novelty entrant, there to give the judges a bit of backchat. So be it.

Since it was prime-time, Saturday evening family entertainment, innuendos were viewed with suspicion, but the BBC couldn't touch me for telling Craig Revel Horwood he wouldn't know a paso doble if he sat on one. And if Tess Daly wanted to tell me I was a 'surprise entry' in the final, how was I expected to respond?

'I like a surprise entry.'

In those days, you did your routine then went back to the dressing room. Nowadays you have to stay in the background and gurn for your money before and after your turn. I wouldn't enjoy that. The studio at the BBC was unfeasibly hot for the live show, the heat building up during the dress run in the afternoon. After dancing and enduring the judges' comments (Bruno: 'The hips didn't move, my darling!' Craig: 'No bounce, no hip action. Flaccid, flaccid, flaccid!') and their miserable scores, I'd be melting. Erin and I would retreat to my dressing room for a post mortem, where Valerie and a bottle of sauvignon blanc would be waiting. The dance-off wasn't part of the format then, and since the public kept voting for us we survived until the final. Having begun feeling indifferent as to whether I would be there the next week or not, I slowly began to enjoy my time on the show and felt a flutter of excitement at the prospect of learning a new dance each week. Erin was a wonderful teacher, the epitome of patient encouragement, and I wanted to please her. Her ambition for me was contagious. As we clocked up the hours in rehearsals I definitely improved, and the hitherto unused part of my brain required to remember the choreography sprang into life.

Valerie had matured into a serene and wise dog, equally at home in rehearsal or dressing room. She liked and understood her role as sentry, and her gentle, watchful nature was perfect for the role. Having watched us rehearse, she would wait patiently in the dressing room while the show was on. She would greet us with a sage nod and a steady gaze when we arrived, panting, after our performance, and we began to communicate through her, as if she were a maiden aunt awaiting our reports of a night on the town.

'Valerie!' I'd cry. 'It's official. I can now dance a foxtrot!'

'Yis,' agreed Erin. 'Diddy only mussed ep two stups!'

Valerie responded to gentle affection and sincere words and would turn away, embarrassed, if displays of affection were too effusive. Valerie's presence by my side, like Fanny's before her, grounded me. She took the place that might, in another life, have been occupied by a supportive, chisel-jawed spouse.

As if they weren't busy enough knocking out outfits for that year's crop of celebs, the *Strictly* costume department made Valerie her own collar each week from the same fabric as Erin's dress, so by the end of the series she had ten, each more glamorous than the last, encrusted in shimmering Swarovski crystals. Against her shiny black coat, these were the height of sophistication. Heads would turn during our walks.

We weren't nervous about the grand final, which was taking place in the glorious Blackpool Tower Ballroom; we knew what a triumph of willpower over talent my presence there was. We were destined to come third, and we knew it. Denise Lewis was an elegant runner up and Jill Halfpenny the deserving winner. We enjoyed ourselves immensely.

As head judge Len Goodman rather neatly put it: 'I think of this competition as a three-horse race. We've got two thoroughbreds and a Shetland pony.'

Bruce Forsyth glanced behind me and added: 'He's wagging his tail.'

Working with the legendary Bruce Forsyth was a career highlight. He made the show funny and exciting, and made sure he had a cheery word and a reassuring comment for all the nervous dancers every week. He showed great affection towards Valerie and often mentioned her during the show: 'Julian now has two women in his life, his dog Valerie and his dance partner Erin. They're both brunettes and both beautiful. But only one of them likes chopped liver and biscuits for breakfast. That's Erin, of course.'

CHAPTER 13

Rustic Life

I was flavour of the month at the BBC for a while. After a quick panto season at the Bristol Hippodrome, Valerie and I were back at the doughnut (the BBC Television Centre) for the weekly live National Lottery Show, the snappily titled *Come and Have a Go if You Think You're Smart Enough.*

It was a Saturday teatime show, and there was the usual BBC nervousness about what I might say. The lottery mafia men in suits were particularly paranoid. I had a scripted line about an item of jewellery: they were convinced that a reference to 'my ruby cluster' was gay parlance for some sinister prostate-stimulating activity, and try as I might, I couldn't convince them otherwise. It had to be changed.

My family history was also investigated for an episode of *Who Do You Think You Are?* As we set off to ask my father about my grandfather, Jack, I removed Valerie's turquoise, crystal-encrusted collar – acquired during our time on *Strictly* – and replaced it with something brown and leathery. I explain to the camera: 'My father doesn't like to see her in glamour-wear.

He gets embarrassed when he walks her around the streets of Swindon.'

In among all this, I found time to write my memoir, *A Young Man's Passage*, diligently typed with Valerie beside me, sighing contentedly. I was no longer interested in going out and dragging strangers home, and writing – this more sedate, thoughtful occupation – was unexpectedly satisfying. My writing routine suited Valerie, I noticed, and I pondered the possibility of less dressing up and flouncing around on stage and a more contemplative, homely lifestyle.

My trips to Mallorca were becoming less frequent, partly because I didn't like to leave Valerie but also because being treated with as much respect as a box of oranges on easyJet lost its appeal. Brighton, too, was not the escape from London I had hoped for. I was complaining about this on the phone to Paul O'Grady one day and concluded that what I really craved was somewhere isolated in the countryside, where I could breathe fresh air and not be blinded by rainbow flags and splattered with semen every time I opened my front door.

I'd known Paul – or 'Savage', as I call him – for many years. Fanny and his dog, Buster, used to sniff each other disdainfully at parties and I can hazily recall an all-night lock-in at the Edinburgh Festival one year where all four of us emerged bleary-eyed into the morning sunshine. Buster was a Shih Tzu/Bichon Frise cross and the most laidback dog I've ever met. 'Not a bother on him,' Savage used to say. During their days on the drag pub circuit, Buster would take himself off to the Gents and cock his leg at the urinal.

Savage was always riotous company, but wise and perceptive with it. Hours would fly by when we were together, and he'd always leave me weak with laughter. He now has a pack of dogs that follow him around like Fagin's pickpocketing gang.

Savage told me there was a beautiful house for sale in the village in Kent where he lived, which used to belong to Noël Coward. Noël! Imagine living in his house!

Our paths had already crossed, in a manner that some might call uncanny and unnatural. I grew up in Teddington, Middlesex, which happens to be Coward's birthplace. Believe it or not, I was a shy, bookish, effeminate child. As I have mentioned, secondary school was not a pleasant environment for me, and I thought it best to be more or less mute once I entered the gates of St Benedict's. Home, in the bosom of my family, was my safe place. There, in keeping with our collective take on life, I would make light of things and turn unpleasant incidents into amusing anecdotes.

At some point in my childhood I became aware of Noël Coward's name. Maybe it was the media coverage of his seventieth birthday (I was twelve) or his death a few years later (in 1973), but I read somewhere that he was born in Waldegrave Road in Teddington, not far from where I lived. I got on my bike and rode past Noël's house and was amazed how similar it was to ours. Intrigued, I investigated further.

Coward's image, his wit, his triumphant career from such modest beginnings struck a chord with me – and my own boyish dreams and ambitions. I read as many of his plays, books and poems as I could find. They were light, funny and anti-intellectual. Just like me. There was something intrinsically gay about Coward's world too. Just like mine.

By the time I went to Goldsmiths, I was a committed Coward fan. And in the student Drama Society production of *Private Lives* in 1980, I played Elyot.

I then went on to do a double act called Glad and May, which featured Fifi and Victor, two ridiculously mannered Coward-esque characters.

Once I left college, my obsession with Coward continued, albeit more obliquely. I felt sure the great man would have approved of the Joan Collins Fan Club, with its elevation of style over content. In the interest of light entertainment I did my best to demystify the shadowy world of homosexual sex with lewd, graphic lessons for the uninitiated, always delivered with perfect diction.

In 1990 a production of *Private Lives* was staged at the Aldwych Theatre in the West End. It starred Joan Collins as Amanda: my two great passions were fused together. When it closed I followed hot on Joan's heels with a six-week run of my own show, *Camping at the Aldwych*. Arriving backstage as the set of *Private Lives* was being loaded out of the theatre, I gave into the temptation to steal a vase. I couldn't help myself. It was a little bit of Joan and Noël to cherish. . .

So when, in 2006, Savage told me that Noël's house was on the market I simply had to go and view it. The two of us went the next day to look at the house. I was immediately smitten. It was a big, rambling cottage with low ceilings, ancient beams, inglenook fireplaces and latticed windows. You could feel Coward's presence in the soot-scented air, imagine him holding forth, dropping *bons mots* like crumbs and composing witty ditties at the piano. Valerie scampered with delight across the acre of lawn and settled contentedly in the shade of a hazelnut tree, as if staking her claim.

'Do you like it, Valerie?' I asked. She gave a slow, contented blink and rolled on her back.

Could I really take on this house, with all its history? Did I think I could cope with the renovations, the responsibility? It wasn't a world I knew anything of. I was a Londoner. I couldn't even change a lightbulb. I'd seen those TV programmes where city types transitioned to become rustic, and they often ended in tears. Savage and I sat drinking tea by the log fire.

'You could sit here all day and just think,' he said.

Valerie wandered over to me and rested her head on my knee.

'Oh, God,' I said through gritted teeth. 'Whatever am I doing?'

In truth, I knew I was going to buy Goldenhurst Old Manor before I saw it, but even so I had to go through the agony of indecision for appearance's sake. I knew what was required of me. The house had me in its clutches the moment Savage told me about it. The survey was forty pages of doom and gloom about various infestations and major concerns, and the conclusion more or less forbade me to purchase such a liability, but it was too late. Nothing could dampen my excitement. In my mind I was already swanning around the house hosting showbiz garden parties and picking flowers. I sold the Mallorca apartment and the Brighton flat, which meant I could buy Goldenhurst and keep my Camden home. There was every possibility I might become one of those dinner party bores who says things like, 'But it's only thirty-four minutes to Ashford from St Pancras on the high-speed train. I can be door to door in an hour and fifteen minutes!'

The reality of the situation didn't really hit me until the day I moved in, a bitterly cold morning in January 2006. I couldn't get the central heating to work and lighting a fire wasn't, I discovered, something that came naturally to me. When I did manage it, the room filled with black smoke. Opening a window didn't seem like a good idea, as they were rotten and hanging off their hinges. Two furniture removal vans squeezed through the five-barred gate, one from Mallorca and the other from Brighton. Men kept carrying in sofas, tables and boxes and asking, 'Which room is this for?'

I didn't even know where half the rooms were or what their function was to be. Luckily my sister Frankie was on hand to take charge while I hyperventilated in the garden with Valerie, surrounded by the blackened heads of last autumn's Michaelmas daisies. Savage arrived with a basket full of eco-friendly cleaning products and a shepherd's pie, Buster meandering behind him. Buster sniffed at Valerie and had a scout round before deciding to christen the house by cocking his leg on an oak support pillar in the lounge. I forgave him when Savage delivered a beautiful Rayburn oven as a moving-in present, which chugged away in the kitchen and warmed the house up wonderfully. Valerie's bed was placed in front of it and she lay there, blissfully content, while Frankie and I cleaned and scrubbed.

A few days later, things were more civilised. We had heating and hot water, curtains at the windows and beds to sleep in. Frankie was good at making lists of everything that needed doing. There was one list for achievable things, like buying occasional tables from the hospice shop in Dymchurch, and another, more sinister, list. It would take years for all the entries to be crossed off:

New roof (house and barn – reclaimed Kent peg tiles only)

Replace oak window frames (retain original latticed glass as
    Noël once looked through these windows)

Replace oak flooring (sounds like rodent activity underneath)

Re-plaster walls (crumbling)

Replace central heating system (doesn't really work and when
    it does flames can be seen leaping from under oil boiler. Also
    relocate – location in cellar under kitchen doesn't seem safe)

Sort out flooding in other cellar

Electrics – rewire house (dangerous, keeps tripping)

Plumbing – replace (leakages apparent)

Garden – find gardener. Plant things other than Michaelmas
    daisies

Replace white picket fence – rotten

Replace five-barred gate – falling apart

I understand that when, undertaking renovations to a listed property, it is wise to get several quotes from reputable companies, but I didn't go in for that. Driving across Romney Marsh one day, I spotted a van with the enticing signage 'BJ BUILDERS' on the side in big red letters. There was my man.

Mr BJ himself had a pleasant manner and nice teeth. 'A lot of people would rip you off, Julian. A rich celebrity like yourself, moving to the countryside . . . but I'm not like that. I won't rip you off. Shall we shake on it?'

BJ and his cheery band of workmen set to work and were a constant source of amusement for someone like me. 'Today I'm going to stick a big, thick pipe in your cellar. I shall be tackling your chimney on Thursday and fiddling with your fuse box by the end of the week. There may be some disruption, but I'll turn you on in a couple of hours.'

The house was, of course, haunted. I knew this, as did Valerie. The joint was jumping with spirits but they were mischievous, rather than devilish. A change of ownership seemed to rouse them to make their presence known: lights would go off and doors would jam so often that we grew accustomed to their funny ways and would simply tut at them and roll our eyes. Valerie would sit, ears pricked, and wag her tail at the residents that she could see but I couldn't. I figured they had been there long before we had and resolved to live with them in harmony – if that meant dispensing with my collection of modern abstract art (the spirits couldn't abide it and flung it off the walls within moments), then so be it. Eventually a woman came with divining rods and wandered through the house, searching for spiritual presences. Turns out there was a seventeenth-century washerwoman in the kitchen, a confused youth in the upstairs middle room, and Noël himself in the front bedroom. Downstairs, outside my bedroom, she discovered a 'vortex' where the spirit of a man called Jack hovered, inexplicably dressed as the Laughing Cavalier. Eventually they all calmed down, only appearing on special occasions to lock someone in a toilet or knock over a bottle of brandy.

I never felt a moment's fear in the house when I was there alone. Rather, I felt embraced by it and calmed whenever I entered. But I was glad to have a dog with me. The house was down a quiet, unlit country lane and there was the occasional muttering about 'Folkestone types' in the village shop. Although Valerie was not gifted in the guard-dog department, the very presence of a canine companion would put prospective burglars off, I thought. Unless they were coming to ravish me by moonlight, there was nothing of any value to steal anyway. Rickety second-hand furniture was what suited the house, and in the unlikely event that Folkestone art dealers wanted my garish modern art collection, currently wrapped in blankets and languishing in a cupboard, they were welcome to it.

There was only one prospective intruder that worried me, and she was a stalker. Everyone who is famous for more than three minutes acquires one of these, and I was no exception. I had a number of 'superfans', and I was always very glad to see them at gigs or in the audience during TV shows: they knew the rules of acceptable behaviour and had no interest in invading my personal space or making me feel uncomfortable. They were there for the buggery jokes and never crossed the line. But my stalker had mad eyes and I knew the moment I encountered her that unpleasantness was coming my way. Valerie knew, too, and would veer away when she saw Alice loitering at the stage door. A signature and a bland post-show chat was never enough for Alice, who wanted more than I could give. Then she started to send me letters, informing me of her troubled domestic situation and urgent need to meet me in private. I began to worry when she turned up on the doorstep of my parents' house in Swindon. She had abandoned her family and moved in round the corner. We could be friends. Or more. . . Could I go for a walk with her? Could we walk Valerie together in Lydiard Park? Her tone was never pleading, but entitled. The more I politely declined, the more persistent she became. She turned up on Christmas Day and my father spoke plainly to her – 'We don't want you coming round. Don't come back' – before slamming the door. To be fair, she didn't return. Not to my parents' house, at least. Alice had other plans. A year later she appeared outside my Brighton flat, smiling strangely, from between some parked cars and handed me a letter in which she said that she'd worked out where I lived from the photo in *Woman* magazine. She also knew my address in London and that she was going to call in some time to check that she was right. Spookily, she asked whether I had wind chimes in my garden and suggested I fixed them to make less noise. She expressed interest in meeting Valerie, and suggested I bring her out for a walk at ten thirty or eleven the following morning.

Then a few months after I moved into the house in Kent she wrote again suggesting she come and stay at Goldenhurst for a couple of nights in early September. She reassured me that she could look after herself and would respect my privacy and wouldn't expect anything – not even conversation. She implored me to allow her the privilege of being a guest in my home and hoped I'd give it some thought. I sought advice from a psychiatrist friend on how best to deal with this and was told that stalkers want attention. If they're deprived of a response, they move on. This is what seems to have happened with Alice. I do hope she isn't reading this sitting outside Christopher Biggins' house. . .

Although BJ Builders didn't rip me off, their labour wasn't free. I had to find work to pay for it all. It was no time to be too choosy, either. Voiceovers for toilet cleaners? I'm in! Corporate gigs for the Bus Shelter of the Year awards? I'll take it! If I had to suffer the indignity of *Celebrity Tipping Point*, then so be it. It would pay for a couple of solid oak windows – and there were a further twenty-two of those bastards to pay for, *and* the French windows. . .

I grew accustomed to the responsibility of the house and rather grandly saw it as my role to bring it back to its former glory. Someone had to do it and I had been chosen, as I saw it, by some form of gay deity. Or something. I settled in and saw that I couldn't achieve everything at once. I had to pace myself and not rush things.

I loved a show I presented for the BBC in spring 2007 called *The Underdog Show*. It was made in collaboration with the Dogs Trust and in it celebrities, including Selina Scott, Clive Anderson and Anton Du Beke, were paired with rescue dogs and had to perform various tests to find out who was 'king of the ring' (I didn't write the script). The heart-warming difference with this show was that all the dogs were available for rehoming, if the celebs didn't take them. Valerie was part of the action too, wafting into the arena with me and looking statuesque as the fancy took her.

But it was clear that the BBC's affection for me was waning when the second series was wrenched from my grasp and presented by Tara Palmer-Tomkinson.

As a result of that show I took my parents to the Dogs Trust kennels in Berkshire to find them a new companion. We looked at all the inmates but none of them quite tickled my parents' fancy, for some reason.

'There is one other dog,' said the kennel maid. 'Suzi. She's a bit special and not yet on view to the public.'

Of course this intrigued us, and we asked to meet her. Suzi was about seven years old, a small black and white sort-of Jack Russell, with huge, swinging nipples that almost reached the ground, like ET's fingers. Her head seemed too small for her body and she had frightened eyes, almost as if she'd been living rough on the streets of Glasgow. Which, of course, she had. It was suspected that she came from a puppy farm and had been thrown out after her pup-bearing years were over. I'm not saying she was ugly, but randy stud dogs must have been blindfolded and force-fed Viagra before being sent into her sleazy kennel to do their duty.

'We'll take her,' said my father. Poor Suzi. She'd never worn a collar or been walked on a lead before. Once she got the hang of it, she would only turn left when out for a walk. Any attempt at a right turn would be greeted with a breakdown, as if she were Ruth Ellis being led to the gallows. Consequently, her walks were rather circular and repetitive, but it gave my father exercise, which was one of the reasons he wanted a dog in the first place. Suzi was friendly with Valerie, even if Valerie peered at her somewhat disdainfully, but she had a great liking for my parents' cat, Meg, and would follow her around the house and into the garden. The reason for this became clear when Meg dug a hole in the flower bed to do her 'business'. What was cat shit to you and me was a tasty snack to Suzi.

'She likes it warm,' observed my mother.

A week later my father had picked up on another of their new dog's eccentricities. 'She seems to be frightened of sparrows.'

Of course, people always say, 'You never know what you're getting with a rescue dog.' But that's true of lots of things, like marriage or biting into a Greggs baguette, for example.

Valerie and I had a lovely summer in Kent. While the builders huffed and puffed over the renovations, I sat on a swing at the far end of the garden writing my first novel, about an unfeasibly well-hung TV personality called Johnny Debonnair who stops at nothing to get what he wants and obligingly knocks off pensioners who have a death wish. I had several titles in mind, including *Dead Man Wanking*, *To Kill a Coffin Dodger* and, my personal favourite, *Catch a Fellating Star*. But one has to be mindful of the supermarket sales these days, I was sternly informed, so it was eventually published as *Murder Most Fab*.

Always one to enjoy a sharp change of activity, I next accepted an invitation to take over the role of the Emcee in Rufus Norris's production of *Cabaret* at the Lyric Theatre, Shaftesbury Avenue, playing opposite Amy Nuttall as Sally Bowles. Nudity was involved but, as my neighbour Paul O'Grady put it: 'It won't be the first time you've shown your arse in the West End.' More worryingly, perhaps, was the singing. I had 'Willkommen' to open the show, not to mention 'The Money Song', 'Two Ladies' and 'If You Could See Her Through My Eyes'. I did my best, but it was always pot luck as to which note would emerge from my quivering mouth. Valerie, I noted, sat through rehearsals with a pained expression on her face and during the seven-month run preferred the tannoy to be turned down in the dressing room. Everyone at the Lyric was lovely, although this mysterious letter I received one day was a little less supportive.

Dear Judas Cunty,

Just a note to inform you that you are a fucking unprofessional twat who has made his name by being limp-wristedly queer and helping to feed a public perception of gay men as *Carry On*-type jokes.

No doubt you'll throw a strop and call on your hangers-on, who you feed with class A drugs and cheap champagne, who will pat your ego, but behind your back, there is not a single member of the cast or crew who doesn't wish to see the back of you for good.

You are a circus freak who has traded on stereotypes all your life. Fanny the Wonder Dog and Valerie are just two of the co-stars you employ to make you look good.

Go back to preening yourself on TV and leave proper actors to make an honest living WITHOUT having to fuck our credibility while you just toss off to your ever-dwindling bunch of sad fans.

I acknowledge that I'm not a singer, actor or dancer. I am a camp comic and renowned homosexual who is sometimes encouraged to stretch himself in unexpected places. This must be galling if you are a bona fide, fully trained exponent of the arts, albeit one understandably eaten up by bitterness and resentment. But it was nice of them to take the trouble to write.

CHAPTER 14

The Unwelcome Visitor

One day I saw in the local newspaper an advert for chickens, and decided that they were just what Goldenhurst needed. But first I needed a chicken house, so I employed someone local to build one. I wanted something camp with a lattice window and a cat slide roof to match the house.

The workman's white van, I noted, had a mini St George's flag fluttering on the bonnet. When he made a fuss of Valerie, he told me he had a dog at home. 'A British bulldog.'

'How nice,' I said.

When the coop was finished, it was the height of chicken luxury and very large.

'You want to be careful round here,' the builder said as I admired his work.

'Why's that?'

'You'll have a family of illegal immigrants moving in if you're not careful.'

I sighed and walked away. I had made him tea but held back

on the biscuits. You don't get a chocolate finger in my house if I suspect you of having right-wing leanings.

I collected six young chickens the next week from a dodgy-looking nearby farm. There were dozens of young hens, all different types, all allegedly good layers. I'd just pointed at the ones I fancied and the farmer grabbed them and put them in a box. Two white (Light Sussex), two brown (Rhode Island Red) and two fluffy Silkies. I called them, collectively, the Nolan Sisters, but gave them all individual names too. Once they'd had a few days to settle into their coop, I bravely opened the door to their run and they approached slowly, pecking at the lawn, keeping together and following one hen, Gucci, who seemed to be their leader. But Gucci wasn't a hen at all. I had my suspicions, as 'she' was bigger than the others with a more pronounced comb. The misgendering error became clear when I heard him crowing at the crack of dawn one day. It was a croaky attempt to begin with, but he soon got the hang of it. There was an unanticipated cock in my garden and no mistake.

I was concerned that Valerie might view the chickens as a snack but, although she was curious, she kept a respectful distance. Eventually they came to her and she let them investigate, pecking her from head to tail as she sat patiently. I let the chickens out into the garden every morning and they sunbathed in the flower beds, made dust baths and were a general, decorative delight.

Gucci grew into a magnificent, protective macho man, crowing, patrolling his gals and, when the fancy took him, grabbing one by the back of the neck with his beak and flattening her, wings flapping during the brief sexual congress. No niceties. No 'How's about it?' I'm not sure it makes it any better, but I'm led to believe that there is no penetration involved with chicken sex. The cockerels just sort of dribble semen in the general direction of the appropriate orifice. But there you go. It wouldn't do for us all to be the same. I've lived in Brighton, so I'm very tolerant of other people's funny ways.

Gucci – snowy white with a grey shawl and black-tipped feathers held high – tolerated me but was likely to rush at Valerie if she dared to move too quickly in the direction of the flock. She learned to slow her pace and keep away.

The hens laid eggs each morning, and I grew to love the 'hen song' – the triumphant squawk they involuntarily make to celebrate the safe delivery of another perfect egg. On summer days, as soon as I woke up I'd slip into my decorative Moroccan *djellaba* and Valerie and I would wander down the path to the coop, a rustic straw-filled basket over my arm, to collect eggs and release the chickens. They would run across the lawn towards the house, overjoyed by their freedom. Maureen (I knew I'd find a home for that name one day), a tiny white Silkie, would become broody every few weeks and remain in the coop sitting determinedly on that morning's eggs, groaning with annoyance when I slipped my hand underneath her to steal them. Sometimes I'd leave them there for a while, as she seemed to be in such a state of catatonic bliss that it seemed unkind to disturb her. Six chickens was enough, I reasoned. I had more eggs than I knew what to do with as it was. No one, not even the postman, passed my house without getting half a dozen fresh eggs forced upon them.

But tragedy was lurking. I'd been out shopping one afternoon, and when I let myself through the side gate I immediately sensed that something was wrong. It was unnaturally quiet. The birds in the trees were struck dumb. No hens came running towards me in case I had a treat for them. No Gucci on guard. Then I saw a sad trail of white feathers leading from the lawn to the fence. Valerie sniffed them suspiciously and turned to look at me. I had been warned that a fox would try to get my chickens one day. As time passed, though, the presence of the dog had put them off. I'd also encouraged my gardener to urinate at will in the garden, as the scent of male urine is allegedly a deterrent. (Obviously this isn't something I could do myself. My celebrity status forbids it and besides, I'm not sure if homosexual urine works. I have no suspicions in that department about my gardener – he's got a tattoo of a naked woman on his back and is a member of an amateur heavy metal band.)

'The fox will be waiting. Watching. Just biding his time. . .' said rustic neighbours, wise to the cruel truth of country living. One of them had a gun. He'd sit up all night if a fox had been spotted in the area, apparently. But it seems I might have disturbed the fox mid-massacre, as not all my chickens had been taken and foxes are not known for leaving a job half done: hidden under a pile of straw in the corner of the coop was a traumatised Maureen. Half an hour later I heard the tentative clucks of more frightened chickens coming from a flower bed next to the house. I called and the two Rhode Island Reds, rigid with suspicion, slowly emerged from among the purple lupins. Valerie, electrified by the fresh scent of fox, raced around doing some uncharacteristically serious barking, sniffing, digging and scratching around the coop and the fence – feeling, I suspect, as if she had somehow failed in her duties. I got the Reds safely into the coop and locked them in.

'The fox will be back . . . he knows there's a tasty meal waiting,' said my cheerful neighbour.

In the kitchen I had the four eggs I had collected from the coop on the morning of the tragedy and decided to slip them under Maureen to see what would happen. They were the eggs from the two dead white hens. If they had been fertilised by Gucci (and who wouldn't want to be?), the deceased would live on in their chicks.

A few days later, after hearing that a fox had been shot in the area by a local farmer, I felt brave enough to let my hens out again – they were wary and far more alert to potential danger – but normal life resumed. Maureen remained sitting on the eggs, just hopping off quickly once a day to eat and drink and do a hefty poo. Then one day, about three weeks later, I heard a faint chirping coming from under Maureen, who chirped something motherly back. I could see the excitement in her eyes, which no longer had a catatonic stare. The next morning there were three little chicks, whose imaginative names were a clue to their appearance: Whitey, Beigey and Browney. Maureen was an exemplary parent, Mother Courage with feathers, watching over her brood and clucking proudly. They grew and grew until they were three times her size, but still she ruled over them. Whitey turned out to be a boy with incestuous desires for his stepmother, so he went to live elsewhere. I acquired two Indian Runner ducks, who I hatched using an incubator and who thought I was their mother. It was all pastoral bliss. I took to wearing gingham and drinking tap water, just like a real country person. By now, I was in my late forties; I can only assume I was trying to find an age-appropriate style. I wasn't getting any younger.

In fact, as I aged I suffered a number of ailments, but annoying as they were I managed to see the funny side. I had policeman's heel, housemaid's knee and something called male prostitute's rectum. I won't go into details but, suffice to say, my heel stung, my knee throbbed and my rectum spat like a ginger tomcat. Gentlemen callers, had there been any, might have been temporarily blinded. Yes, age is a terrible thing. I had to face the fact that I was all aches and pains and leakages and dribbles. I needed to settle down and live a nice quiet life in my country house. I needed love. I needed someone to cuddle up with on the sofa watching daytime telly, someone to enjoy a pork chop with of an evening, and someone to ejaculate over the *Radio Times* with on a Friday night. I was just like everyone else in that respect.

Rolf had returned to England by now. Although we were an item, his job was all-consuming. I think it was in an office, but I must confess I tended to glaze over whenever he talked about himself. All I knew was that he worked all the hours God sent. I'd be in bed when he left at seven each morning and back in bed when he returned at midnight. There was a six-month period where he never once saw me standing up. I was just a prone figure under the duvet and a wisp of mascara on the pillow. It must have been like living with the Turin Shroud.

In order to express my dissatisfaction in a creative and lucrative way I did a tour called *Position Vacant, Apply Within*. In the second part of the show I selected ten men from the audience ('Hang the risk of MRSA') and with the aid of a cattle prod herded them on stage and 'auditioned' them for the coveted role of my husband ('For one of you, life is going to change overnight. You won't be able to walk in the morning'). The nonsense concluded with a fake marriage, complete with wedding dress and a blessing from a bishop.

'I can't wait to get you back to my hotel, the White Swallow. Will you be gentle with me? We've got half an hour before my Viagra kicks in.'

It was all, of course, a thinly disguised plea to Rolf to firm up our relationship and fully commit to me. It worked like a dream, I'm pleased to report, and he tore himself away from his modest flat in Stockwell and moved into my luxury celebrity home(s). One promise I made to him was the imminent gift of his own dog. He loved Valerie, and she him, but we had room in our lives for another. He wanted a pedigree Italian greyhound which he planned to call Saveloy. Unfortunately, fate had other plans.

PART THREE
Albert

'Dogs will save humanity . . . they're made of goodness.'

Ricky Gervais[8]

CHAPTER 15

Urges on Daytime TV

Rats. Anyone who keeps chickens knows that rats aren't far away. They mean no harm, of course – they're just after the free food. Country rats look clean and healthy, too. They don't hang around sewers and that sort of thing. I'd seen the odd suspicious burrow in the vicinity of the coop and caught a glimpse of 'things' dashing for cover as I approached, but when I lifted up the ducks' paddling pool one morning and found a squirming pink nest of newborn rats, like salmon sushi with peppercorn eyes, I realised I had to do something. I wasn't running a rodent takeaway at the bottom of my garden. Like many a city person before me, I was disturbed by the visceral goings-on of nature. I might tut at a shoplifter in Camden High Street, or shake my head at a bloody crime scene, but if I saw a headless mouse in a hedgerow or a fox predating my chickens, I was in need of counselling, and possibly sedation.

It so happened that on 9 May 2009 I was a guest on *The Paul O'Grady Show* to promote my second novel, *Devil in Disguise*. The other guests were McFly, the burlesque performer Immodesty Blaize, and three homeless puppies.

As I said to Savage during our interview, 'Fancy having me on with homeless puppies and McFly. There's no way I'm leaving this studio without a new special friend.'

The truth was, I'd already met the puppies backstage and one in particular had made my heart beat faster.

'Do you fancy one?' asked Savage.

'I've had a look at them and I'm beside myself.'

In the final part of the show, the floor manager, Ossie, brought on the puppies.

'These three are all looking for a new home,' said Savage into the camera. 'They're Jack Russells crossed with something – we don't know what 'cos the dad's done a runner.'

A telephone number flashed up on the screen for anyone who was interested to call. A wave of anxiety washed over me at the thought of a viewer calling and laying claim to 'my' puppy before the end of the show. I thought I should act fast.

'Can I hold him while you do your next interview?' I asked the host, trying not to sound desperate. Savage handed him over and smiled. He knew there was one less homeless puppy in the world.

While Savage chatted to Immodesty I sat and stroked the sleeping brindle puppy. This time there had been no slow build-up of need. It had come in a rush, an unexpected tsunami when I woke up that morning. After the show, I took him to my dressing room, where he sat on the carpet like a chunky little frog and looked at me curiously as if to say, 'Me? Are you sure about this?'

He had an amused, laidback air about him and his tail wagged sloppily from side to side.

'Do you want to come and live with me?' I asked, giving his

Left: Yes, well, I think we get the general idea.

Below: My parents with Bonnie and Zara

Above: Albert as a puppy.

Above: It took a while to win Valerie over but eventually she succumbed to Albert's charms.

Left: Maureen and Albert were great friends.

Left: Nick in the garden at Goldenhurst

Below: With Savage. His Bette Davis to my Joan Crawford.

Valerie surveying her garden at Goldenhurst.

Rolf's affection for Albert is unseemly.

Valerie and Albert knew the Panto script better than me.

Embracing rustic life: I even drank tap water sometimes.

The Joan Collins Fan Club meets Joan Collins.

Rolf and Joan have fun with celery.

Rolf slipped his finger in my ring at last.

Left: Gigi in transit from Serbia to a new life with a renowned homosexual.

Below: Gigi masters the camp pose

neck a gentle scratch. He sniffed my hand then rolled on his back, as if knocked out by my kind offer.

I wanted to take this delightful dog home with me that day, but the people from Teckels Animal Sanctuary explained that I couldn't do anything that reckless. I had to think about my commitment to the puppy and call them the next day. Impulsive theatrical types were viewed with suspicion, quite rightly. (If I treated my dogs the way I treated my gentlemen callers, the Battersea Dogs Home would need a much larger premises. I'll say no more.) Only then, if I was sure I still wanted him, could I arrange to go to Teckels in Gloucester to fill out the adoption paperwork. I was petrified that he'd be given to someone else in the interim, but they assured me he would be 'reserved' for me. They called him Albie and he came from a local group of travellers – two facts which any homosexual will confirm only made him more attractive to me.

There were only two immediate issues I had to deal with, and I was sure they'd come out in the wash, as it were. First, there was Valerie. She had little time for puppies and would curl her lip when they approached. Her serene nature didn't sit well with excitable play or rough and tumble. Apart from Queen Latifah, she seemed to find public displays of affection embarrassing and she would stiffen and look worried when they were initiated. She liked a gentle stroke and a nuzzle and I predicted that the constant company of a playful puppy would be her worst nightmare. I discussed this with the person from Teckels when I called and they seemed to think the dogs would work things out between themselves but, if not, then Albie would have to be returned.

Second, there was Rolf and his promised Saveloy. He'd seen me on *The Paul O'Grady Show* and objected to our abandoning the original plan. No amount of enthusing on my part seemed to dispel his disappointment. I had been selfish and done what I wanted and conveniently forgotten my promise when it suited me. A ginger mongrel with stumpy legs was a far cry from the elegant Italian greyhound Rolf had expected. *Was this what life with me was going to be like?* he wondered. Everything on my terms, my celebrity whims negating his own wishes? And on and on. There were a lot of unanswered phone calls.

But there was no going back. My feelings for Albie were no less strong for being sudden and unexpected. I had no doubt in my mind that this dog was destined to be a source of joy in my (and hopefully our) life, and I ploughed on with the adoption plans. Valerie and Rolf would come around, surely. All would be well.

On the appointed day, I left Valerie with my parents and drove to Gloucester with my friend Nick to collect Albie from Teckels, a small, well-run and happy charity. I filled in the forms and made my donation and was then led to a pen where Albie was running about with four or five other dogs. The kennel maid told me he was a lovely, well-adjusted boy, but quite assertive. I'd need to keep him in check as he had a tendency to get carried away. They had trained him to respond to a sharp 'Ah!' sound from the back of the throat – this meant 'Stop whatever you're doing!'

'You might find it useful,' she said casually as she handed him to me. I held him tightly. He seemed pleased to see me and was just as gorgeous, heart-melting and full of character as I remembered. He sat on Nick's lap wrapped in a towel for the journey back to Swindon, curious about everything going on around him but not in the least bit worried.

Once we arrived we put him on the lawn. Valerie sauntered towards him, peering down at the new curiosity, looking somewhat horrified. He yelped and jumped up at her. Valerie turned on her heel, strode into the house and refused to come out again. Having, it was thought, extensive experience with puppies from her days incarcerated at the puppy farm, my parents' dog Suzi was much friendlier, joining in the play fighting and allowing Albie to climb over her and pull at her ears.

A few hours later Nick went back to London on the train and I drove to Kent, Albie asleep in a cardboard box on the front seat. Valerie sulked in the back, wearing an expression of mournful disgust that no cheerful chatter from me would shift. I had a couple of days alone before Rolf was due to come down. Valerie remained aloof. If the puppy came into the room, she would leave. When he waddled up to her in the garden she'd snap, and if he persisted she gave five or six sharp barks in his face, the subtext of which was an expletive-filled demand to leave her alone. He'd back away, bewildered, shake his little head then sit down to look at her, plainly wondering what he'd done wrong. If they had eye contact she'd bare her teeth. Stay away!

I'd never seen her so cross and upset. She was never keen when other dogs came to visit but I hadn't seen her this furious and filled with contempt before. Albie, all innocent mischief, seemed to forget about her reaction after a few seconds and bounced fearlessly back to Valerie for another attempt at rough and tumble, which was greeted with higher-intensity canine obscenities. I was a bit worried and made sure Valerie had time alone with me when Albie was safely in his crate in the kitchen. I sat with her and gave her some tender, therapeutic strokes and words of reassurance.

'He's only a baby. He means well. You're number one still. Don't look so worried.'

She didn't seem convinced and let out a shuddering sigh. Any sound from the crate and she'd glare, showing the whites of her eyes as if a volcanic eruption were imminent. She seemed relieved when bedtime came and we went upstairs, safe from the puppy. In the morning Albie would be ecstatic to see her and she'd be aghast, hoping his existence had been a bad dream.

I decided to get Albie used to the chickens as soon as possible. He was young and playful, and bounded up to them full of curiosity, only for them to squawk and flap and scatter. I didn't want them upset, as well as Valerie and Rolf. I kept them in their pen and several times a day carried Albie in. Whenever he looked at a chicken I said, 'Ah! No!' very firmly. After that, when I let them out and Albie so much as glanced in their direction I said, 'No!' again. It worked. From that day on, Albie looked through the chickens as if they weren't there, completely ignoring them. When he was older he'd chase pigeons (and sometimes catch and kill them), but he treated chickens like invisible ghosts. He'd let them sit next to him, steal his biscuit, even, but he'd pretend not to see them.

I was nervous the Saturday morning Rolf was to arrive. The atmosphere during our brief telephone conversations had remained minty. He and Valerie were besties and I was imagining a scenario where they might unite against me in their distaste for Albie. It could be a difficult weekend.

I sat on the front lawn with both dogs, listening for the sound of Rolf's car coming down the lane. Valerie sat stiff and stony-faced, her back to me and Albie, while I did my best to stop him pestering her. He clambered over me like a lion cub, amusing himself with his own waving tail, then with the buttons on my shirt. He was a happy pup and his personality was that of a cheeky Cockney barrow boy, effortlessly charming and confident. He waddled in front of Valerie and rolled on his back, legs splayed, pawing the air under her chin, trying everything in his power to appeal to her, but she curled her lip and turned away. He sat up and moved into her sight line again, head tilted to one side, and let out a little yelp of frustration. I offered her a treat but she wouldn't contemplate it. She winced and stared at the gate, waiting for her saviour to arrive.

When Rolf finally parked on the drive and called her she ran, leaping and shrieking, into his arms, as if she were starring in a re-enactment of the Cleveland kidnappings. Then it was Albie's turn. He hadn't quite got the hang of sprinting yet, so he kind of bounced across the lawn, tail wagging, full of excitement to greet someone he'd never met before. With Valerie in one arm, Rolf scooped Albie up into the other. The adoration was instant. Luckily for Valerie, love is not finite. It grows and expands – and there was plenty to go around. Half an hour later Rolf was on the sofa, Albie asleep on his chest, and the room, the house, if not the entire county of Kent, was glowing with contentment. I allowed myself a little sigh of relief. Everything was going to be all right.

But while Rolf was instantly won over by the new family member (he could hardly bear to be parted from him), Valerie was not so easily seduced. Her revulsion was downgraded slightly over the next week to something resembling intense dislike, but Albie wasn't allowed to come anywhere near her without angry objections on her part. But he never gave up. He'd look at her longingly, ignore her growls and try to lick her, wait till she was asleep and then jump on her. He was fearless. I don't know if he was familiar with the poetry of John Donne, but his technique was remarkably similar:

> Licence my roving hands, and let them go,
>> Before, behind, between, above, below.[9]

Eventually it paid off. Suddenly, with no preamble. One afternoon, about three weeks after Albie's arrival I was cleaning out the chicken run when I saw movement in my peripheral vision. I turned and saw Valerie and Albert rolling around together on the lawn in ecstasy. She had thawed out in a nanosecond: detachment had turned to affection, irritation to coquettishness, enemy to friend. I was astounded. Had she secretly liked him all along? Had she been playing hard to get? Had she been shy? Perhaps dogs need to establish a pecking order to live alongside each other harmoniously.

Whatever the reason for Valerie's sudden decision to accept Albie, it made for a much happier life for everyone. When they weren't playing together they would settle down to rest side by side, greet each other when they had been apart, and sometimes just sit in companionable silence. No more frowning and sulking, thank goodness. I had grown tired of Valerie wandering around with a face like a smacked arse.

Having a younger dog around also seemed to give her a new lease of life. At almost ten years of age she was slowing down a bit, and keeping up with Albie's youthful exuberance made her fitter and more fun-loving. I knew how important this was. I was about to turn fifty myself.

Fifty! It's a difficult age. Too old for alcopops, too young for *Midsomer Murders. . .*

CHAPTER 16

Drugs! At My Age!

In Noël Coward's day Goldenhurst was famous for the fabulous parties Noël threw, attended by the great and the good. Coward might have had Laurence Olivier, Vivien Leigh, Katharine Hepburn and the Duke of Kent wafting around the lawn, but for my fiftieth I managed Immodesty Blaize, Kenny Logan and Jo Brand. Savage came too, so I made sure we had plenty of cheap cider in.

Other guests (there were about a hundred) drank pink champagne served by (I specified) good-looking waiters. I also had some portaloos installed in the garden so the gays would have somewhere private to take their drugs. Much like in Noël's day, I suspect.

Over the next few months Albie (whose name had slowly evolved into Albert) began to fill out. And out. He bore no more a resemblance to a Jack Russell than I did. He couldn't catch a ball, let alone a rat. We slowly realised who the 'father who did a runner' must have been: a Staffie.

'You promised me an Italian greyhound,' said Rolf, stroking a sleeping Albert. 'What have I got? A ginger Staffie!'

I phoned Savage with my complaint. He said, 'Sorry. No refunds' sharply and hung up.

Oh well. Too late now.

I met up with Nick one evening to talk about Albert's progress. That was the pretext, anyway. The truth was, I was worried about him. He hadn't looked well when we went to collect Albert, and as his oldest friend I thought I should be the one to deliver some plain speaking. As it turned out, I didn't need to. He arrived late at the restaurant, swaying in the doorway, glowing buttercup yellow, his stomach swollen, his trousers tied with string. We abandoned dinner and, despite his protestations, went straight to hospital.

When the doctor asked how much he drank, he replied, 'Just the occasional Wellington boot full of sherry.'

His liver was failing. Over the next few days, litres of ascitic fluid were drained from his abdomen. Very close to dying, he clutched at life and managed to keep hold.

This was the beginning of his long, but spectacular, recovery, involving expert medical care, counselling, Alcoholics Anonymous and steely determination on his part. Over the next few years it was wonderful to see the old Nick return, as witty and wise as he had ever been.

'I now have the liver of an eighteen-year-old,' he declared, and began an MSc in psychodynamic psychotherapy at Birkbeck College. Four years later I proudly watched him graduate. This was a triumph in the face of adversity if ever there was one, and Valerie greeted the new, sober Nick with genuine enthusiasm, just glancing briefly behind him to check that his demons were gone for good.

As you get older, certain things become unseemly, like wearing cap-sleeved T-shirts in your thirties, going to gay nightclubs in your forties or taking drugs in your fifties. Being married to an abstemious husband helped in regard to the latter, and I had long since given up my sniffing and snorting habits. This sacrifice was helped, I maintain, by the deteriorating quality of the stimulants on sale. In the 1990s cocaine was very pure. It was practically a health food. You'd take it to clear up your sinuses and ward off colds, coughs and flu, while a gram dissolved in water and used as an enema provided instant relief (and may account for the mid-1990s craze for pebble-dashed walls).

I was alone at Goldenhurst one evening, scribbling away, dogs asleep contentedly beside me, when there was an unusual occurrence. Nothing much happened in the village – if a sheep blinked, it was an event – so at the sound of a speeding car and a distant police siren all three of us leapt up to look out of the window. No sooner had the car passed my twitching nets than I heard the screech of brakes and a sinister thud. A police car passed seconds later. This was drama of the highest order. I went out to the gate to see what had happened, but whatever it was had occurred just around the corner by the nearby woods. A few hours later, a neighbour called to tell me what it was all about. Apparently, some ne'er do well youths from Ashford (local shithole) had stolen a car and come joyriding through our peaceful village. They'd misjudged the bend and, by divine retribution, ended up in a ditch. The police arrested them and they were now in custody with a new offence to add to their doubtless lengthy rap sheets.

The next morning was bright and sunny, and I took the dogs

for their usual walk in the woods. I saw the tyre marks on the road leading to the ditch and the flattened hawthorn and holly where the car had ended up. I tutted and walked on. Then I stopped. What was that I'd just seen? I turned back for another look. Yes. There it was. A tiny plastic bag nestling in the nettles. It was about two inches square – the sort of bag you might get buttons in at a haberdashery. I picked it up and saw that it didn't contain buttons at all, but a small quantity of white powder. Albert and Valerie were keen to get to the woods and chase the squirrels so I didn't hang around. I slipped the packet into my pocket and climbed over the stile.

As I wandered through the sun-dappled trees, everything suddenly became clear. I had drugs in my pocket. The Ashford youths, finding themselves in a ditch with the police hot on their heels, had acted fast.

'Quick!' one of them had no doubt shouted to his chums. 'The pigs are coming! Dump the stash!' The desperate lad had chucked the bag out of the window in the nick of time.

The police had then come and taken them and the stolen car to the station. As the first eagle-eyed passer-by I had, purely by chance, found myself in possession of at least half a gram of Ashford's finest marching powder. As a lapsed Catholic, I'm always on the lookout for a sign from above and here one was, as plain as the (excitedly twitching) nose on my face. A benevolent force had seen from above that I was struggling to write some top-notch comedy and had delivered a little something to help. Cocaine would get my comedy juices flowing, as sure as eggs. Praise be!

Although my drug-taking days were behind me, this was a

gift from God that I couldn't refuse. Just this once, for old times' sake. No one need know.

The dogs' walk was cut a little short that morning as I rushed home to do the good Lord's bidding. In my kitchen I retrieved the plastic bag from my pocket and had a closer look. Definitely cocaine, I concluded. I'd know that white powdery texture anywhere. But it was a little damp after a night in the ditch, so I spread it on a Pyrex dish and popped it in the Rayburn on a very low heat to dry. While this was going on, I fed the dogs and got my pen and notebook ready. If everything went according to plan, I should have some class A gags in the bag in time for elevenses. I took the powder out of the oven and placed it carefully on the breadboard to cool while I rolled up a twenty-pound note. It was just like old times. Valerie wandered into the kitchen and gave me a questioning look.

'It's all right, Val,' I said. 'I'm just doing what needs to be done in the interest of light entertainment.'

I prepared myself a modest line, gave thanks to Kerry Katona and snorted it hungrily.

It took me about five seconds to realise my mistake.

'Shit,' I said, grabbing a tissue and blowing my nose as quickly as I could. But I was too late. My sinuses began to burn and my eyes watered. It wasn't cocaine at all. I'd experienced this sensation many years before in a club in New York. I'd just taken a hit of crystal meth.

I was furious. I mean, it was ten o'clock on a Tuesday morning. One minute I was minding my own business walking my dogs in the Kent countryside and the next, through no fault of my own, I was high, floating on the ceiling with eyes like saucers and feeling sexual stirrings of a most unsavoury nature.

The time in New York wasn't my fault either. I'd arrived in the Big Apple two hours before and had gone straight to a club someone had recommended, called Hot Cock For Men. I had been in a queue for the Gents when the man behind me tapped me on the shoulder and discreetly handed me a compact mirror with a not over-generous line of powder on it. I only sniffed it to be polite. I can remember the horrible burning sensation in my sinuses, which I attributed to jet lag at the time. The next thing I knew, I was doing unspeakable things in a multi-storey car park with a man who looked like Mr Bean. (I'll spare you the details, but it involved a rolled-up copy of *Marie Claire* and a tin of Swarfega.) It was only when I read an article in a magazine on the flight home about the crystal meth epidemic gripping the NY party scene that I realised I had been scurrilously deceived and used as a plaything to satisfy the base lusts of a man I wouldn't normally have nodded to, let alone exchange body fluids with.

This time I managed to keep myself nice. It was quite easy in an empty house in the middle of nowhere. I'm only glad the vermin control man didn't turn up.

Dogs sense when you are off-kilter, whether it's due to chemical enhancement or the flu. They don't judge, just sit quietly with you until the malaise passes, a grounding presence, there to pull you gently back to reality. I once ate a spoonful of magic mushrooms preserved in Manuka honey at a party in Belsize Park in the early 1980s, and had such a bad time on them that I can't think about it even now without feeling ill. I found myself in an altered reality, walking among the dead. If Fanny hadn't been by my side, concerned, licking, peering into my dilated pupils and calling me back, I might still be there now.

As it happens, this time I got off lightly and the whole sorry incident made me more determined than ever to lead a clean, green life from now on. I like to think I've succeeded. These days, out of consideration for my poor abused body and the welfare of our planet, I don't drink, I don't smoke, I don't take drugs, and I've cut right down on my breathing. When I have sex I use a biodegradable mint-flavoured condom. I use it and then pop it into a salad. No need for any dressing. Perfect.

The show I had been trying to write when I was so rudely interrupted by drug-crazed urges was called *Lord of the Mince*. It was a success, so more dates were added, and then some more. There were almost a hundred performances in the end, and the dogs came with me to most of them. Valerie and Albert had no objections to being in the car, lulled to sleep as soon as we got on a motorway, and they seemed to be enlivened by daily walks in a different town every day and the new smells and friends they encountered. They snoozed in the dressing room during the show and waddled on during my encore to gladden the hearts of the dog-loving punters. It was a routine of sorts – travel, theatre, hotel – and I like to think they found it stimulating. They were never bored. They got to know the country and its theatres, from Truro to Stirling, and I imagined they had a streetwise swagger when domestic life resumed.

The panto season each year was another time when they got to know a new, exciting world – although I'm not sure Crawley, where we performed in 2009/10, could, in all honesty, be called exciting. We stayed in a serviced flat above a giant Asda store, which was as glamorous as it sounds. The good news was, there was an excellent dog-walking trail behind the theatre. Even so, with two shows a day I employed a professional local dog-walker to take them out for an hour during the matinee to wear them out. Someone called Malcolm came each day and picked them up from my dressing room. After a few days I noticed Valerie came to sit under my chair whenever Malcolm arrived. The next day I decided to walk them outside to the car park to try to put her at ease. The problem became apparent at once. Malcolm was transporting the dogs to a nearby field in crates in the back of a van. When he opened the double doors, I saw that there were six other dogs in individual crates, stacked on top of each other. Albert couldn't wait to be lifted in, but this was far too rough and ready for Valerie, who looked like someone who was about to be forced into a mud-wrestling competition.

A crate! Other dogs! A field! I made her excuses and after that Albert went off alone for his hour of rough and tumble with Malcolm and Valerie enjoyed some quiet time in the dressing room.

Dog walkers are generally very pleasant, trustworthy people, and Valerie's problem with the service Malcolm offered was no reflection on him. But we'd had problems before. I'd employed a woman to see to Valerie's exercise during panto one year, but Valerie returned each day with injuries allegedly incurred while out walking. This can happen, as we know. A bruise, a scratch . . . but a cut on her inner thigh, apparently from jumping over a fence and landing on a stick? It looked like a remarkably neat cut to me. The vet stitched her up and said he thought it looked like a knife wound. I let the woman go before things escalated further. Munchausen syndrome by proxy, I suspect. The Beverley Allitt of the dog-walking world.

There was another man from an agency in London who seemed a little odd. When he rolled his sleeves up to put the dog's lead on I noticed self-harm scars up his arms, and I also spied a gimp mask in his Tesco carrier bag one day. These things didn't put me off; whatever he did in his private life was not my business. He was great with Valerie and she liked him. The reason I stopped using him was more mundane: he didn't turn up on several occasions. He 'forgot'. I dare say you lose all track of time when you're zipped into a PVC mask hacking away at yourself with a razor blade. So I 'forgot' to employ him.

Albert's original purpose was to catch rats around the chicken coop. This he never achieved. It may be that the aversion technique I employed to stop him harming the hens drove any thoughts of catch-and-kill from his mind while in the vicinity. But elsewhere he had no such qualms. He'd kill pigeons and pheasant. When we strolled across neighbouring fields he caught several rabbits, dispatching each instantly with a fang through the top of their skull. He then brought them to me and laid them at my feet. Clearly hunting was 'in his blood'. I assume he may have been bred for the purpose by the travellers of Gloucester, his antecedents providing the meat for dinner made to a traditional recipe involving wild garlic and nettles. Or so I imagined.

This would explain Albert's bewilderment when I greeted

his delivery of the dead rabbits with horror, putting him on the lead to prevent more carnage and leaving his trophies behind for another predator to find and consume.

Albert was less successful with squirrels, who would leap to safety with a millimetre to spare then turn and mock him, sitting just out of reach in the mulberry tree in the garden. He would sit there for hours, staring longingly at them. The next day he would resume his vigil at dawn, obsessed with the one that got away. We've all been there. Valerie, being longer of leg, was more successful, once grabbing a squirrel by the tail. She was so surprised at her luck that she immediately let it go.

At night Albert would carry his toy squirrel to bed with him and fall asleep with his jaws clamped over its face, twitching every few seconds, dreaming of the ecstasy of the kill. When he wasn't in hunting mode, Albert was calm and loyal. Although it has to be said, he grew up to be a curious-looking dog. People would often stop and ask, 'What is he?'

He was compact and muscular with short legs, the front pair turned outwards like the balletic supports of a Queen Anne footstool. Apart from his white paws, chest and snout, he was a striking brindle tiger stripe: dark ripples, sometimes breaking into dashes and dots, on a red base, with every variation from mustard blonde to chestnut orange. He was a little pungent, in a Staffie sort of way, but we have learned to live with it. His black nose is always wet and shiny and his expression curious, willing to please. He's interested in what you're thinking, always reading you for a sign of what you'd like him to do for your amusement. Roll over? Fetch something? Make curious grunting noises whenever you break eye contact? Just say the word.

Albert would fit very nicely into a stereotypical East End pub scene in the 1950s. He'd sit happily all evening at the feet of a flat-capped, beer-drinking old man, eat the pork scratchings that were tossed his way then lead the sozzled old boy back to his rented home at closing time. The fact that Albert found himself the companion to a renowned homosexual who wafted around his country manor wearing a kaftan, who made unseemly amounts of money telling buggery jokes, didn't bother him at all. Albert went with the flow.

One of Albert's great pleasures was visitors. While Valerie was wary (though not unfriendly), Albert greeted any visitor with boisterous excitement, jumping up, sitting on their lap and pressing himself against them as if they were the person he'd been waiting to meet all his life and he'd like to come to live with them at their earliest convenience.

This was all good fun, of course, but I was expecting a visitor who would not welcome this behaviour. My former namesake, the global icon, film and television superstar and style guru Dame Joan Collins and her husband Percy were coming to stay for a weekend of refreshing country air and poker. Dame Joan was always nervous around dogs. Call me psychic, but I saw trouble ahead.

CHAPTER 17

Albert is Aroused by a Dame

I had met Joan briefly when we were guests on *This Morning* a few years back. It hadn't gone well. My catchphrase at the time was 'Please don't touch me', so when Ms Collins came on the set and sat next to me, that's what I said. She didn't know I was joking and there was no time to explain before the cameras rolled. Our brief encounter was consequently a little on the frosty side.

So when we were cast in a production of *Dick Whittington* at the Birmingham Hippodrome in Christmas 2010, we more or less picked up where we left off. Joan was playing Queen Rat and I was Julius, the Spirit of the Bells. In other words, she was evil and I was good. Relations were brittle, on stage and off.

QUEEN RAT: And what would it take to get rid of you? A forklift truck, I would have thought.

JULIUS: Listen to her, boys and girls. Isn't she dreadful? Why don't you boo her?

QUEEN RAT: Silence, you horrible children! If you're not

careful, I'll come down there and frighten the living
daylights out of you!

JULIUS: Don't take any notice of her. She'll never get down
there without a Stannah stairlift.

QUEEN RAT: Look who's talking! He's had so much Botox
that the only expression he can register is rigor mor-
tis.[10]

But over the run of the panto, we relaxed. Our dressing rooms
were next door to each other, so daily greetings – and my open-
ing-night gift of some glittery silver eyeshadow – helped us to
thaw out. I stood in the wings each day and watched her first
entrance – in a revolving giant Fabergé egg, dressed in a black
diamanté basque – in awe. She was charisma and stage presence
made flesh. Joan threw fabulous champagne-fuelled parties for
the cast and crew in private hotel rooms, danced with everyone,
and spread her stardust generously around. At one such gathering
she asked me about the Joan Collins Fan Club and I explained
that it was a tribute to her, not an insult. This wasn't entirely true,
but she wasn't to know. We are both Gemini, so we like things to
be fun and light. We like a laugh. We discovered our shared love
of cards and Joan offered to teach me poker, which she did. By
the end of the run I felt as if I had been taken under her wing,
and we promised to keep in touch.

'Come to Kent!' I said, not thinking she would accept my
invitation. But she did.

I had a few weeks to prepare, so I cast a critical eye over Goldenhurst. I told my gardener Andrew the date of our VIP visit

and he set to it, making sure every flower would be in bloom and every weed removed. The chickens were bathed and the coop given a spring-clean. The dogs were washed and brushed. A lorry-load of new gravel was delivered for the drive, a man employed to linseed-oil the beams and freshen up the stucco with exactly the correct shade of jasmine cream, and to paint over the mud splashes on the white picket fence. The lawn was to be freshly mown, twice, the morning of their arrival. And, of course, I sent Rolf for anal bleaching.

Our interior furnishings were, I could now see, not good enough. I had made do with a mish-mash of furniture from my Mallorca flat and Brighton apartment, not to mention various bits and bobs from charity shops. None of this would do for Dame Joan. I took a deep breath and feverishly embarked on a complete makeover. Out went the saggy orange sofas and in came new regal purple ones from Liberty. Grubby rugs were thrown out and new ones purchased. New curtains were fast-tracked. Joan's room was redecorated and antique linen sought. I bought towels from Harrods. What if Joan wanted to watch TV? I sent for a new, the-biggest-you've-got, top-of-the-range flat screen TV. What if she wanted to read a book? I went to Foyles and bought a lorry-load of bestsellers (first editions only). I visited nearby Rye and found a gorgeous dining table and chairs for Joan to dine on, then purchased table linen, cutlery and a dinner service for her to eat off. I bid for – and won – a sturdy vintage card table at an auction and found a luxury engraved poker set, counters and cards online. Gravel was raked, windows were cleaned, stairs were hoovered, white orchids tastefully placed on every table and Diptyque black fig candles lit in every corner of every room. Pine-scented logs crackled gently in the inglenook fireplaces. I agonised over menus (Joan is very keen on coronation chicken and chocolate mousse) and my friend Nick, a former chef, came to do all the cooking and serve drinks (including rosé wine – chilled and very dry with an ice cube). I even arranged for amusing guests (famous and/or rich) to pop in unexpectedly so I would look like a popular and well-connected host. Finally, everything was ready. I had spent thousands, but it was worth it so long as my humble home looked acceptable to Dame Joan.

Minutes before Joan and Percy were due to arrive, I made a final inspection. Excellent. Even the weather was behaving. Shafts of spring sunshine beamed decoratively through the spotless latticed windows, illuminating the now-tasteful interior to perfection. I breathed a sigh of relief. Valerie, as if sensing she must be on her best behaviour, sat daintily on a cushion in the corner of the dining room. But where was Albert? I eventually located him in the garden. In a flower bed. He'd chosen this moment to bury his squirrel toy among the delphiniums, which he had flattened.

'Albert!' I called crossly and he came to me, tail wagging with delight and caked in mud from head to foot. I swear there was a glint of roguish satisfaction in his eye.

'Look at you! What have you done?'

There was no time to bath him so we gave him a wipe down with a damp Spontex and sent him to be shut in the kitchen in disgrace while I did my best to prop up the delphiniums with bamboo sticks.

I heard the toot of a car horn and the sound of a Mercedes

pulling into the drive. My guests had arrived. Trying to appear relaxed, I wafted casually through the side gate to greet them. Their Louis Vuitton bags were spirited away to their suite while Joan and Percy made appropriate remarks about the house and garden.

'You must take us as you find us.' I sighed. 'I barely had time to put the hoover round for your visit.'

'Dog,' stated Joan as she passed a placid-looking Valerie on the way to the lounge for refreshments. 'Very well behaved. Don't you have two?'

'Yes, Albert is around somewhere,' I replied, raising my voice to cover the ominous whimpering from the kitchen. We chatted as we tucked into our sandwiches (with the crusts cut off), but after a few minutes we were interrupted by Albert rushing into the room. He'd escaped and was anxious to greet the visitors.

'Ah. Albert's here,' I said nervously. 'He's . . . quite young.'

Albert gave Percy a cursory sniff then made a beeline for Joan.

'Ugh!' exclaimed Joan. Albert jumped on the sofa and pressed himself to her side, tail thumping with friendly delight as he gazed lovingly up at her.

'This always happens,' said Joan, shaking her head. 'I'm nervous of dogs, but they always want to be my best friend.'

'He definitely likes you. Very much!' declared Percy, raising his eyebrows. I followed his line of vision and there it was: Albert was sporting a huge, pink erection.

I thought it best to lure Albert back to the kitchen with a biscuit before he ejaculated over the Victoria sponge.

'He can't help it,' I explained. 'You're a very charismatic woman. Just be grateful I don't have a pet goat.'

CHAPTER 18

Celebrity Big Bucks

Life at Goldenhurst inspired my next novel, *Briefs Encountered*. Its main character, an actor called Richard Stent, had recently bought the house and explained to the reader:

> Like a wealthy businessman under the spell of a beautiful Jezebel, I signed the papers and prepared myself, willingly, to be fleeced . . . It's not a house, bear in mind, but a monument, host to all who have dwelled within its walls, a saturated rag of damp, breathing spirits.

This is rather flowery talk, but a true enough statement of how I felt. Life there with the dogs, chickens and ducks was blissful but the cost of the renovations was eye-watering and there was no end in sight. It wasn't a 'lock up and leave' weekend cottage. I couldn't pop to the village shop without a mysterious flood happening in the basement or a swarm of hornets arriving to take up residence in the roof. I needed to keep the coffers full to pay for it all, and showbiz life is notoriously fickle. Ask Angus Deayton. I had plenty of work – panto paid well and punters turned out to see me on tour – but one false move and it could all evaporate. I was in my fifties, and I was starting to feel a bit like I was chasing my tail.

So when my agent called me in 2012 with the offer of appearing on *Celebrity Big Brother*, my ears pricked up. There's only one reason anyone enters the Celebrity Big Brother house – and that's cold, hard cash. I could say I was curious too, and you might believe me. I'd watched every series since my pal Davina told me she was going to be the presenter. The celeb version was excellent car-crash TV fodder, and I was hooked. Now it was relegated to Channel 5 and Brian Dowling was the new host, but the format was the same. The public perception was that any celeb taking part must be in desperate need of the loot, or exposure to fertilise their dwindling career prospects. In my mind I dressed it up as easy money that I needed to do up Noël Coward's stately home, a mission I had undertaken for the cultural benefit of the nation. But this didn't appear to wash with some.

'How low can you sink?' asked one friend, aghast. But the fact remained: an awful lot of money could be mine, and all I had to do was be locked in a house with a volatile mix of celebrities and obey Big Brother's rules.

I sat in my lounge thinking about it, listening to rats scuttling about under the ancient floorboards and an ominous dripping from the basement.

Quite low, I decided, in response to my friend's query. My

fee would pay for everything the house needed, and I would be worry-free. I called my mother.

'Just say yes,' she said. So I did.

The only problem was that I had a tour booked to start a week after the *CBB* run, so we rehearsed the new show before I went into the house and hoped that I'd remember it when I came out.

Because all the housemates were to be a surprise – to the public and each other – a day before the show began I said a fond farewell to Rolf and the dogs and was spirited away to a hotel in Elstree. I checked in wearing a balaclava and dark glasses. My mobile phone was confiscated and my luggage searched for any hidden devices – and, I guess, illegal contraband – and I was locked in a bedroom. Runners with walkie-talkies led me down to a studio for official photos and interviews then back to my room for a psychological assessment, to make sure I would cope with the strain of what lay ahead. Apparently, the psychologist can always predict from these interviews who will win.

The next day was the big launch. After hours in make-up and dressed in a jaunty black and blue polka-dot suit I found myself on set with the baying crowd and the host Brian Dowling, having a few cheery words before I entered the Big Brother house. I knew what was expected of me.

'What I'll bring to the house is a bit of class and a very tight sphincter,' I informed him. 'I'm planning to have sex in the jacuzzi within the first twenty minutes. If necessary, I'll have sex with the jacuzzi.'

My housemates were Julie Goodyear, Martin Kemp, Coleen Nolan, judo champion Ashley McKenzie, journalist Samantha

Brick, MC Harvey, actress Cheryl Fergison, TV personality Mike 'The Situation' Sorrentino, Prince Lorenzo (me neither), model, actress and bad gal Jasmine Lennard and glamour girls Rhian Sugden and Danica Thrall.

You know how it works. It's a bit like *One Flew Over the Cuckoo's Nest* but without the anti-depressants. Days are spent doing wacky tasks or sitting around in the garden, chain-smoking. Big Brother manipulates things to create conflict: there are parties and punishments, flirtations and feuds, losers and winners. I fairly quickly worked out that, from twenty-four hours of film, the editors had to make a one-hour TV programme, so as long as I said or did one or two interesting things a day I could sit quietly for the rest of the time and watch the goings-on while others exhausted themselves being constantly 'on'.

I had been dreading sleeping in the communal dorm, but apart from feeling claustrophobic when the doors snapped locked each night, it was fine. I slept next to Julie Goodyear, a childhood idol of mine, and it's fair to say we shared a similar camp sense of humour. She has that feisty northern attitude that I've always found fascinating.

I had strange, arousing dreams. One night I dreamed that Julie leapt on me. She crawled under my duvet and started humping me. I could feel her womanhood through my pyjamas. When she rolled off me I rolled up my pyjama leg and there on my thigh was a suction mark: the distinct outline of Julie Goodyear's vulva.

The series was not without upsets – that's what we were there for, after all. Jasmine called Danica a prostitute, Ashley and The Situation (who I referred to as The Occasional Table) got the hots for Rhian, Sam called me 'emotionally a cold fish' (I was thrilled) and Coleen and Julie took a dislike to each other, so it was handbags at dawn. But none of this is worth recalling. It was light entertainment for the nation and we were happy to provide it.

I had a difficult few days when the feeling of being trapped (which of course I was) became overwhelming, but I didn't let on. I reassured myself that if I really wanted to leave then I could. If you bolted, though, you'd only be paid pro rata, depending on how many days you'd been in. So, as I lay in the garden with a flannel over my face, I worked out my daily rate. Hmmm. Worth suffering for, I decided. Funny how the thought of a new boiler and a top-of-the-range cast-iron guttering system can perk you up.

The 'letters from home' featured in the last week. Mine was from my mother.

Hello Julian,

I'm so pleased to get the opportunity to send you a message. I know how you worry about us. Everyone is fine. Your father is making good progress and can now manage to take Suzi for her daily walk. We all miss you, of course, and it's strange not to have your phone call each evening although we do get to watch what you're up to on TV.

Thank you for the flowers, which arrived after you went into Big Brother. I'm going to try and keep them going until you come out, but I'm starting to need a smaller vase each day.

Everyone I've spoken to sends lots of love, and that includes family, friends and people from the Bowls Club. Last week I had a four-hour lunch with friends and I only had a smoked salmon sandwich.

Much love,

M.

I missed being alone with Albert and Valerie, and worried about them. Big Brother (who I came to acknowledge, was master of everything) must have sensed this need. After we had all competed in a story-telling challenge, there was an announcement: 'This is Big Brother. Julian passed this task with flying colours. Julian has therefore won the chance to get his hands on a lovely pair of puppies.'

I was then called to the Diary Room, where Valerie and Albert were waiting to see me. We had ten tearful minutes together. It was rather like a prison visit – but I couldn't resist one thing.

'I need to blow a raspberry on Albert's inner thigh. It's a private matter, if you wouldn't mind, Big Brother.'

'What did Valerie and Albert think of your story-telling?' asked BB.

'They've heard it all before, Big Brother, frankly. They're sick and tired of the constant references to buggery and oral.'

My visit from the dogs cheered me up immensely and I sailed through the rest of my 'time' and then won, if you please. God bless the British public for voting for me. To my surprise, this reduced me to tears as I'm not used to winning anything. I sobbed uncontrollably on Coleen Nolan's chest, and not many homosexuals can say that. Walking out, last to leave the house, with the cheering crowds and the fireworks, confetti and media frenzy was quite overwhelming. As soon as I could, I phoned my parents.

'Don't let it go to your head,' advised my mother. 'I know it looks like it, but you haven't become President of the United States of America.'

She wasn't wrong. The excitement lasted about three days, then everyone forgot my triumph and life returned to normal. But am I glad I did it? I am really. I'd never won anything before. I just wish it could have been for achieving something. I did nothing. I just sat there for three and a half weeks being homosexual. Alex Reid can do that. The experience gave me an idea for another reality TV show: eight celebrities are locked in a house with no lavatory. The last one to soil themselves is the winner. It's called *Big Bladder*. What do you think?

Then, after a few glorious days at home with Rolf and the dogs, I was off on tour. First stop Barnstaple. It was sold out, and with a much younger crowd than I was accustomed to, thanks to my recent TV triumph. This didn't stop me serving them the usual gratuitous filth.

I opened with a song called 'The Homo Mambo'. 'It's been a few years since I took up a Latin American.'

It went something like this:

> *Pluck those eyebrows, zhush that hair*
> *Then press your Ginger Rogers to his Fred Astaire.*
> *Go, go, go commando*
> *When you dress for your Homo Mambo!*

While I was away, my odd-job man came to Goldenhurst to put the chickens away one day and interrupted the fox indulging in another spot of carnage. Two of the chickens and the ducks were gone. Only a traumatised Ahmeda and Maureen had survived. The odd-job man took them to the safety of his house for a few days until I was home, then he arrived with them in a cardboard box. I sat with them in the coop as they were released. They stood stock still for a minute or two, then looked around. Pecked and sniffed. Then something extraordinary happened. They cried. Both chickens stood and screeched, a pitiful, heart-rending scream I'd never heard them make before. Albert and Valerie bowed their heads, as did I.

Ahmeda was a lovely chicken, fat and friendly, with red plumage – she'd hatched from one of the eggs Maureen had brooded. She and Maureen would come and sit by me when I was in the garden and settle in the shade underneath my sun lounger. Maureen liked to perch on the sill when the French windows were open, but Ahmeda came into the house and would follow me into the kitchen in search of crumbs. When I was working she'd hop onto the desk and sit watching me.

If I lifted her up she'd settle contentedly on my lap and go to sleep while I stroked her.

A year later, I noticed her droppings had become watery. Her feathers appeared dull, her comb pale and floppy, and she seemed to be losing her plumpness. I wormed the chickens, added cider vinegar to their water and gave Ahmeda a course of antibiotics, but nothing seemed to help. Her poop remained alarmingly watery. The vet said she was fading away. She carried on for several more weeks until one morning she was lying on her side, her eyes closed, struggling to breathe. I said my goodbyes and called my neighbour, who knew how to deal with the situation quickly and painlessly. Poor Ahmeda. She basically shat herself to death. Poor Maureen – all alone. But she didn't seem to mind. She blossomed. Being the smallest of all the flock, she'd always had to fight her corner and, wily and fast as she was, I'd noticed she was bullied somewhat, even by those she'd hatched out of the kindness of her heart. Maureen now had a new lease of life, queen of her own domain. She attached herself to Albert and would sit quietly by him or at the French windows watching me.

She developed an intense liking for mashed potato too. She was a very happy chicken and would live to see her twelfth summer. Old age got her, not the fox.

Talking of old age, we had a family house party that year. My Auntie Tess skipped into her hundredth year so seventeen Clarys, aged from one to a hundred, came to pay homage, sleeping on every available surface. Auntie Tess, fit and fierce, had all her marbles about her and a few to spare. We had a chat one afternoon, sitting under the fig tree in the sunshine, Maureen, Albert and Valerie snoozing beside us. She had recently taken up darts, she informed me.

'Are you any good?' I asked her.

'I don't know. I haven't hit the board yet!' she replied and hooted with laughter.

One of my nieces made her a fancy pink and white birthday cake and after she blew out the candles I asked her what she had wished for.

'For another year,' she whispered. She got her wish, and another few years besides, dying two weeks before her hundred and fourth birthday. She was found dead one morning in her kitchen beside a broken saucer, a dustpan and brush in her hands. It's what she would have wanted. Her ashes are buried in the garden at Goldenhurst under a flourishing scarlet rose tree called 'Hope for Humanity'. We tend not to go for a lingering death in our family. Best to get it over with. Auntie Wynne died on her way to the shops – she keeled over and fell into a hedge, dead before she hit the privet. My grandfather died after stepping into the porch for some fresh air. My grandmother called out, 'Let me go!' and passed over, minutes after being admitted to hospital.

Then there's all the 'stuff' to deal with when someone dies. It took me weeks to clear out Auntie Tess's flat. She had saved everything. I suppose you never know when you might need a receipt for a bag of nails purchased in 1946. I remember, when I was flat-hunting in Brighton, being shown a flat in Brunswick Square. The estate agent explained that the previous occupant had been an old lady who died suddenly while out shopping. Only distant relatives could be traced, who wanted a quick sale, contents included, so they could divvy up the proceeds. Everything was just as the old lady had left it that fateful morning: a bone china cup and saucer on the draining board, a Vladimir Nabokov novel, splayed open to the page she had been reading, next to her reading glasses on the bedside table. Even her fluffy slippers in the hall, faithfully waiting for their mistress to return. Now it was all to be sold, got rid of.

When a dog dies, there isn't much to dispose of. Just a bowl, a bed, some toys and a collar and lead. But not many of us can throw away the lead. It hangs, limply, on the back of the door, all purpose, all life drained from it.

CHAPTER 19

Valerie's Trouble

Valerie was showing her age. Her athletic trot became more of a trudge, her coat wasn't as shiny, and she was afflicted with strange, fleshy growths on her face. To begin with I mistook them for ticks and, I'm ashamed to say, tried to pull them out with tweezers. Her pleading expression caused me to think again and the vet explained that they were warts. Not attractive, but nothing to worry about. She still ran about with Albert but he was now faster.

Still beautiful and composed, Valerie maintained her sphinx-like serenity, albeit a little chipped and weatherworn. She would lie in the sunshine, her head on her paws, thinking wise thoughts. If she was to be stroked it must be gently, head and shoulders only. Any touch of the nether regions or, heaven forfend, her tail, and she would look round with alarm. If you persisted, she would move away a short distance and settle with pursed lips. She didn't care for loud music or chatter, and if subjected to either would leave the room. She was more Claire Bloom than Claire Sweeney.

One day, alone at Goldenhurst, I was at the kitchen sink,

rinsing some courgettes. It was a warm day so I had all the doors open. I could see Valerie wandering about the drive by the barn doors. She seemed to be going in circles but with her head down between her front legs, somehow. Maybe she was chewing on something? Or had something stuck between her teeth? I decided to investigate.

When I reached her, I realised Valerie was in distress. She didn't seem to be able to stand up properly and was staggering around, her eyes juddering from side to side. I thought she might be having some sort of fit. I swept her up in my arms and took her inside and laid her on a rug and held her, trying to calm her and comfort her. I could see she'd been sick all over the house, too. Maybe she had been poisoned? A wasp sting? I needed to get her to a vet, so I called Farmer Fay who lived a few minutes away. Fay looked after the dogs and chickens for me sometimes and was a kind, practical animal-loving person. By the time she arrived I had rather gone to pieces, sure that Valerie was dying in my arms.

'I think she might have had a stroke,' said Fay as she dialled the vet's surgery. 'I've seen this eye movement before in some of the older dogs I look after.'

We left a worried-looking Albert home alone and drove to Ashford. My hysterical tears, which took even me by surprise, abated somewhat during the journey and I was a little more in control of my emotions by the time I rushed Valerie in to see the vet. She examined Valerie and explained that she had canine idiopathic vestibular syndrome. The disease comes on suddenly in older dogs, causing loss of balance, disorientation, head tilt and irregular jerking eye movements known as nystagmus. It is similar to a stroke, but not the same. Some dogs make a full recovery, but often the head tilt and some restrictions in movement remain.

'We'll need to keep her here for a few days for treatment,' she said gently. So far I had listened and nodded sensibly, stroking a quivering Valerie all the while. But with the news that Valerie would be hospitalised – separated from me, confused, sick and her future uncertain – a wave of emotion swept over me again, tears sprang into my eyes and my sobbing filled the room.

'I'm sorry,' I managed to say, embarrassed that I wasn't able to control the sobbing and whimpering. I expected better of myself. A little sniff or a moist eye may have been acceptable in a fifty-four-year-old man, but I was a blubbering mess, consumed with the idea that I would never see Valerie again and that her death was imminent.

The vet handed me a tissue and spoke kindly but firmly. 'I know it is a shock and her symptoms look very dramatic, but I have treated many dogs with this condition and the vast majority make a good recovery. She needs anti-vomiting drugs and sedation and then she will feel better. Don't worry. The nurses will take very good care of her.'

I then had to say goodbye to Valerie – and yes, it was a little like the deathbed scene in *A Farewell to Arms*, where Helen Hayes departs for the afterlife and whispers to Gary Cooper, 'Don't let me go . . . in life and in death, we'll never be parted . . . I believe it and I'm not afraid.'

Fay led me out. I shuffled through the waiting room, blind

with tears, then she took me home to Albert and a sink full of unwashed courgettes.

It's remarkable how cleansing a good cry can be. Such a release! I resolved to do it more often, if only to clear my sinuses.

I tried to limit my phone calls to the duty nurse at the animal hospital to four a day, although I did call in the middle of a sleepless night to verify the twenty-four-hour care claim. Valerie was doing well, responding to treatment. Yes, she had eaten her special food. Yes, she was managing to sleep. Yes, they were stroking her head and scratching her ears regularly, as instructed. Yes, they were sure she was missing me, but she was coping with the separation.

After four days I was allowed to collect Valerie and bring her home. I had medication to administer and the vet, pleased to see me dry-eyed and not in need of smelling salts, told me she was on the road to recovery. I was beside myself when she was led into the room. She walked slowly, head tilted firmly to one side. She stood still for a moment, peering at me, then wagged her tail furiously, the effort of which caused her to lose her balance and keel over. I went to her and helped her onto her feet. She pressed her head into my hands and we closed our eyes with the bliss of being reunited.

'It's all over now, Val,' I told her. 'You can come home.'

Albert, who had looked high and low for Valerie during her absence, glaring at me accusingly – he seemed to be convinced I'd left her in the car – greeted her with boisterous adulation. She licked him back in her self-conscious way, walked stiffly around the house and garden, inspecting all her old haunts, then settled herself in her favourite spot in a shaft of sunshine in the study and, with a sigh, fell into a contented sleep.

Valerie was remarkably accepting of her compromised condition, but it took me a while to catch up. This was a new phase of her life. No more athletic sprints and leaps. Her playful moods were few and far between, and when she did find herself succumbing to a spot of rough and tumble with Albert she let him do all the work while she more or less lay there, just jerking the odd limb in the air to show willing. And the playfulness didn't last long before she put a stop to it, pulling herself together and removing herself from the situation with a haughty sniff. When we went out in the car, she now stood patiently by the open door waiting to be lifted in. Getting onto the sofa was a hit-and-miss affair, as were her toileting needs. I've always had a kind of psychic knowledge of when my dogs needed to 'go', but these twinges failed me now. Valerie had lots of accidents, and I could tell from the look of embarrassment on her face when she walked into a room that a pile or a puddle had just been deposited.

Despite the vet's prediction that she'd make a full recovery, Valerie's head-tilt stayed with her. If she sneezed or shook herself, she'd collapse in a heap like a binge-drinking lass in a documentary about nightlife in Grimsby. Further assessments by the vet revealed she also had canine cognitive dysfunction – doggy dementia, to you and me. Just like Fanny, she had become old before my eyes. She was now unsteady and forgetful, prone to staring into space and spending her days quietly in a darkened downstairs bedroom. She would totter in to find me every few hours, maybe do a wee – in the garden, if I opened the door in time – and return to her solitude. It was a bit like living with an incontinent monk.

Carpet stains aside, I have a great fondness for old dogs. There is a website called Oldies Club (https://www.oldies.org.uk/) that I've spent many a happy evening perusing. As the name suggests, the organisation matches saintly dog rescuers with the elderly dog of their dreams. Such as Max, an ancient three-legged terrier:

> His best days are clearly behind him and he has a few health issues. He can't be left alone, will need to sleep in your bedroom, doesn't want to be picked up or have a cuddle. He has forgotten his house training so has puppy pads down in each room. He doesn't like strangers or cats and he isn't happy in a car. He enjoys going out in his buggy, eating and sleeping.[11]

Don't all rush.

But Valerie accepted her new circumstances, so I did too. Her life had changed but was not over. There was life in the old dog yet. My own life revolved around ensuring she had a comfortable old age. She was no longer up for bracing walks along Dymchurch beach or a couple of hours tramping across Romney Marsh. Instead I led her slowly around the village green or along the Royal Military Canal at West Hythe, a short drive away. It was a pleasant walk but there danger lurked – in the form of the Most Boring Man in the World: 'Good morning, Julian, my friend. It started out nice, didn't it? Then it turned. I took one look out the window and I said to my wife "You'd better get the washing in, I think there's going to be a shower".'

Why didn't he get the washing in himself? Even Valerie would glaze over, and she was only half there in the first place.

Then it was home to boiled rice and chicken and her medication cunningly concealed in dollops of organic yoghurt, before a nap.

By a cruel twist of fate, we encountered the Most Boring Man in the World quite often when out with the dogs. He'd see me before I saw him and it was usually too late to change course. . . He liked to talk, at length, about British wildlife. He didn't do normal conversations. He talked in anecdotes. Long ones, and it was impossible to extract yourself until he had finished. You then had a very brief window of opportunity to escape before he began another. One theme was seals.

I was on the beach in Norfolk, Julian, with my wife, and I couldn't believe my eyes. Thirty yards away, there it was. A seal! And once I was in Scotland. I was watching a fisherman. He was catching salmon as they swam upstream. He had one, and half its face was missing. I said, 'What happened?' He said, 'Look over there, near the far bank of the river, and you'll see.' I looked and looked and I couldn't see anything. I looked again. Nothing.

By this time of course, I knew what the punchline was going to be. A seal. I nodded knowingly but the Most Boring Man in the World was enjoying his moment.

The fisherman said, 'Keep looking.' I must have been there seven or eight minutes. 'Over there!' he said. But I was flummoxed. 'You'll see it when he closes his nostrils,' said the fisherman. I couldn't think what he was on about. Then these ripples appeared and I saw something glinting in the water. An eye. It took me a while to focus as the sun was shining. And then I saw it. Well, blow me. A seal!

This was my opportunity to wrap up the conversation and escape.

'Well, goodness,' I said. 'I'd better be—'

But I was too late.

'And there was another occasion when I was a young man swimming off the east coast. . . What do you think I saw?'

A camp comic wielding an axe?

Old bores aside, I tried to make life as comfortable as possible for Valerie in her old age. Obviously, it no longer suited her to come with me on theatrical trips. Her dressing room days were over, so I made arrangements for dog-sitters to stay at Goldenhurst and tend to her special needs. Rolf was working in London and couldn't oblige. Over Christmas 2013 I was in *Jack and the Beanstalk* in Cardiff, giving my best to the role of Spirit of the Beans, so a lovely woman called Abbie came to stay for the season. Abbie was writing a book, so a quiet six weeks in the countryside with just two dogs and a chicken to look after suited her nicely. She spent a couple of days with me getting to know the ropes before I departed for Wales. It all worked well, and she sent me nightly emails informing me of the goings-on, Maureen's activities and the dogs' bowel movements.

Late one morning in early January I was getting ready to go

to the New Theatre for the two o'clock performance when my phone rang. It was a number I didn't recognise, but I decided to answer.

'Do you have a dog called Valerie?' asked a well-spoken man. 'Is she lost? Only we've just found her wandering along the street in Hythe.'

Panic-stricken, I explained that Valerie was my dog but I was in Cardiff. Please would they hold on to her while I called Abbie, who was looking after her in my absence? I promised to call them back as soon as I found out what was happening. Abbie was distraught when she answered. She had been walking the dogs by the canal when Valerie disappeared. There had been heavy rain for days and the bank had eroded away. She was convinced that Valerie had fallen in and been swept away. . .

No, she was safe, I reassured her. She had found her way to the street somehow and had been found. I'd call her back once I'd spoken to the man. He wasn't far away. Valerie would be back with her in two minutes. Wait in the car park. But the well-spoken man wasn't two minutes away. They had their son in the car who was in a rush to get to Heathrow Airport to catch a plane to Canada, so they hadn't been able to wait. They were sorry, but Valerie would have to come with them and they'd drop her off later if I could give them the address. Valerie was asleep on the back seat and seemed fine.

I didn't like to tell them about her weak bladder. Poor Valerie. Poor Abbie. Poor well-spoken man. Poor me, so helpless and so far away, struggling through a dreary matinee, tortured by thoughts of my demented dog thundering down the M20 without her breakfast, her well-being dependent on the kindness of strangers.

She was returned to Abbie's arms at 5 p.m., cross-eyed with confusion but none the worse for her adventure. I sent the well-spoken man some flowers as a token of my gratitude and Abbie kept Valerie on the lead during future excursions, which she seemed to find comforting.

CHAPTER 20

Life Gets Better – and Worse

It had taken a lot of time and effort, but the refurbishments to the house and garden were more or less complete. BJ's work was done. There was always something, of course, this being rustic life: a badger moved into the basement for a while, the barn wall spontaneously combusted thanks to ivy growing through the windows, the five-barred gate fell off its hinges in some sort of cry for attention. But generally, I was free to enjoy the fruits of other people's labours. My gardener had done a splendid job planting the country cottage flowers that I wanted, and on summer evenings as I sat on the lawn with the dogs, sipping a gin and tonic, surrounded by white roses, pale hollyhocks and pink geraniums, listening to the birds in the trees and the sheep in the nearby fields, I thought I might cry with happiness. What could I do next to make the house even more perfect? The main thing I had to figure out was balancing my work with Valerie's needs. She didn't like travelling any more, either by car or train. She was an old dog and any interruption to her daily routine unsettled her. A succession of friends and relatives who came to stay each time I was required to work elsewhere wasn't a satisfactory solution. The answer, I realised, was a live-in housekeeper. Eureka! Someone homely and who loved animals who could look after the house and dogs for me. There was a corridor of rooms, complete with a bathroom and sitting-room, where he or she could live separately from me. Imagine the luxury of not having to clean, iron and shop for myself any more!

I found an agency that deals with such matters in the back pages of *The Lady* and put aside a day to interview the applicants. This wasn't easy. Not only did I have to imagine living under the same roof as this person, but I also had to trust them and like them. I interviewed four women. Some were strange.

'I want you to confide in me. I won't just be a housekeeper, I'll be your friend.'

Another informed me that her fourteen-year-old daughter would be living with her. 'And she will be having her friends around. You can't expect otherwise with a girl of her age.'

In the end I chose a nice, clean-looking woman called Hermione who had short red hair and rosy cheeks. The dogs took an instant liking to her and I approved of her no-nonsense Glasgow accent and easy laugh. Furthermore, she'd previously worked at Kensington Palace so was obviously comfortable in the presence of homosexuals.

To help her, I presented Hermione with some handy notes about the animals.

Valerie

Sixteen-year-old mongrel. Deaf. Unsteady on her feet. Enjoys a quiet life. Responds well to stroking and a fuss. Sixteen months ago suffered episode of peripheral vestibulitis. This is why her head tilts to one side. She has been a bit 'special needs' since then.

V'S ROUTINE

Wakes up early to go outside. Then back to bed.

Short walk @ 9–10 a.m. (coat on if cold or wet). She is v slow – likes to sniff a lot. Not particularly keen on other dogs. Put her on a lead near ponds or canals in case she topples in. Rub down with (red) towel after if she's wet or muddy.

Food when you get home. Then she usually goes back to sleep until lunchtime. Out to garden again. Wanders about aimlessly sometimes, maybe give her a chew. . .

Dogs can have an afternoon walk if you want one, but not necessary.

V starts wanting her food @ 3 p.m. but hold off till 4.30 p.m.! Then she usually sleeps for a few hours. Several outings to garden (half a gravy bone biscuit after).

Watch her with a torch after dark.

Make sure she doesn't eat plants (she's particularly fond of the plants at end of garden by by the swing – but they give her the runs).

Last outing @ 10 or 10.30 p.m.

Sleeps in your bedroom.

Albert

A six-year-old Staffie/Jack Russell cross. Easy-going, healthy, affectionate. Quite lazy.

He fits in with V's routine but likes to chase around the garden (particularly at night). Obsessed with next door's dog, so barks over the wall. Needs to be stopped if goes on too long. . . He often barks at other dogs when out for a walk. Can be a bit aggressive with small dogs or puppies but has never had a fight of any sort. Quite protective of V.

Keep them both on the lead if you're worried.

A. will sleep on your bed given half a chance, but just as happy downstairs on sofa or by Rayburn.

Chicken

Maureen – white Silkie. Agile, healthy. Seven years old. Glynn (odd-job man) cleans her out and changes straw every Wednesday. Add extra straw if it gets cold. She doesn't lay eggs at her age.

Let out in the mornings @ 9 a.m. She will peck around the garden – comes when you whistle or offer some chopped-up apple or leftover potato or whatever is going (not too much). Put away any time after 2 p.m. She should follow you if you have food. Two handfuls of mixed pellets and corn (in barn). Check water. If raining hard or snowing, put away earlier or don't let out at all. She has a nice large run.

There is a danger of a fox attack while out. It's only happened twice in seven years, and there's nothing we can do about it anyway.

With Hermione at the helm, Goldenhurst took on a new *Upstairs, Downstairs* vibe, although who was up and who was down was open to debate. I had to discuss menus with her once a week and she wasn't shy about giving the gardener and odd-job man their orders. While Rolf and I sat by the fire reading the Sunday papers she would appear in the doorway wearing a pinny and say, 'Is there anything I can get for you gentlemen?' then reappear with a drinks tray and cheese straws. She amused us endlessly. There's something very comforting about being told 'I've got some nice Jersey Royals on the boil.'

Hermione would put us in our place too. One day she'd had her roots done in Hythe in the afternoon and, to protect her hair from absorbing cooking smells, served us our dinner with her head wrapped in cling film. We hooted with laughter.

'I'm not here to be made a laughing stock of, gentlemen,' she snapped. We fell silent, like naughty schoolboys.

I was away quite a bit, filming a series for ITV called *Give a Pet a Home*, hosted by Amanda Holden. Filmed at the RSPCA's Newbrook Farm Animal Centre in Birmingham, it involved 'celebs' helping animals of every shape and size to find their 'forever home'. If you wanted a pet rabbit, Peter Andre was your man. A dog? Coleen Nolan had a lovely selection. Kittens? Denise Lewis would show you round the cattery. An added thrill for the viewers was that the celebs might fall for a rescue animal themselves and whisk them away to a life of luxury. Coleen took home a Shetland pony and a three-legged terrier, and Peter Andre left with a Staffie. I was in love with a big ginger tom called Jeremy, who I thought would look delightful sitting on my windowsill in Kent, but by the time I'd made my mind up he'd been claimed by a family in Acocks Green. If only he'd waited. . .

It was all quite heart-warming, as I recall, although we did have to wear hideous purple fleeces, as if we were bona fide Animal Centre employees. I felt a bit like a Kwik Fit fitter. Plus I had to share a loo with Chris Kamara. A career highlight, I'm sure you'd agree.

I can only think that someone in the Factual department at ITV liked me, because I was then asked to attend a meeting about a new series called *Nature Nuts*.

The idea was to travel around the country meeting people who were obsessed by the wildlife in their back garden and beyond. With an expert film crew, boasting some of the UK's most talented natural history camera operators, I would play fairy godfather to these nature nuts by capturing their favourite creatures in ways they had never been seen before. The camera team had all the latest technology on hand to capture animals in their natural habitat. In fact, there wasn't much left in the budget to pay the presenter, but how about it?

Was I allowed to be funny? Yes, they were all for it, although it was to be a Sunday teatime show, so hold back on the fisting gags. A comedy nature documentary? I could feel a new genre coming on.

I left the dogs with Hermione and off we set in search of kestrels in Yorkshire, otters in Sunderland, beavers in Scotland, hedgehogs in the Midlands and seals in Tyneside. It wasn't a glamorous project. When I asked about lunch, I was told we'd 'pick up a sarnie at Tesco later', but I got used to it. My clutch bag was bulging with savoury snacks by the end of the first week. I even travelled in a car with velour seat covers. I just didn't care. Because I'd toured so often, I knew the country well, but only cities and towns. With this series I saw glorious countryside, met delightful, eccentric animal lovers, and improvised comedy nonsense with my faithful camera persons and sound persons, who I constantly misgendered as Maureen and Susan. I loved every minute and thought the finished product was, after being involved with so many forgettable shows that were barely one rung above closed circuit TV, the best thing I'd done for years. As I said in the opening scene, 'I haven't been this excited since I got locked in a horse box with Prince Harry.'

As Sam Wollaston at *The Guardian* rightly surmised:

> To be honest, I don't think Chris Packham needs to worry or look over his shoulder too much; JC probably doesn't have the seriousness or expertise to be a proper threat. He does have the laughs and the lines, though. My favourite – a willow tree described as 'the Magaluf of the owl world'. And the lesbian bats.

I thought I'd found my niche, and would have happily done *Nature Nuts* for the rest of my days. The camera-work was amazing, the programme showed a deep and genuine love for animals, and we had laughs along the way. I had high hopes for another series. But in the cut-throat world of television, I guess the viewing figures weren't good enough. Someone, some-where, turned their nose up and the series was unceremoniously dropped by ITV. I believe I used the C word when I was told.

I returned to Kent to lick my wounds. As Coward once remarked in his diaries, the 'house and garden seemed to embrace me'. Hermione made me comfort food, Valerie and Albert were pleased to see me, and Rolf and I decided to plan our secret wedding. That cheered me up.

My accountant pointed out sternly that there was a lot of money going out of my bank account and not much coming in. What should I do? I had a fear of ending up like Dale Winton, who died in April 2018 in a rented house in a north London suburb, his money all gone. I'd better not go on living beyond my means.

So it was off on the road again with my latest tour, *The Joy of Mincing*. To get myself in the mood I had a look on YouTube to see what other stand-ups were banging on about. I sat in front of my computer with a cup of tea and some peanuts. I wondered what was going on out there. I might get inspired.

Simon Amstell. He had a lot of angst. Talked about how lonely he was. Very funny stuff. But I couldn't do that. I had no angst. I wasn't lonely. Far from it. I had to lock myself in the toilet for a bit of me time. (And even then I often was not alone.)

Stewart Lee was 'riffing' on Colin Powell and the Middle East situation. Hilarious. Award-winning. But I felt I had nothing to contribute there. I wish I did. Unless you want to know about the huge Arab cock I managed to accommodate in the souks in Marrakesh in 1984? Maybe not.

No, my public didn't want angst and politics. I had better stick to what I had been getting up to of late. There was a lot to tell my punters about. Me and Joan together in the South of France:

We liked to sit watching the sun go down. She showed me photos of her former lovers – Warren Beatty, Dennis Hopper, Harry Belafonte. And I showed her a Polaroid of a lorry driver I met in a bus shelter in Wolverhampton.

My recent foray into the world of children's literature:

Recently, as some of you may know, I have minced into print as a children's author [show book]. The Bolds are a family of hyenas who want to have social intercourse with human beings. God knows where I got that idea from. But there's a chance that when I was young I was held down and ravished by a hyena. It wasn't uncommon in Teddington.

This is my first book, *The Bolds*. The sequel, *The Bolds to the Rescue*, is out in March [2016]. And I've just finished the third book in the series, *The Bolds Decide to Try Double Penetration*.

And, of course, poor Valerie and her vestibular disease:

So, Valerie now has a twenty-four-hour care package. There's a St Bernard at the bottom of her bed with a barrel of brandy round its neck in case she gets lost. A troupe of performing border collies comes in once a week to amuse her. They're rubbish. I can walk on my hind legs better than they can. And because Valerie can no longer manage to eat her own

vomit, a boxer comes in and does it for her. I think his name's
Mike Tyson.

While I was on the northern leg of the tour, Valerie's condition
took a turn for the worse and Hermione took her to see the vet.
Hermione's email to me sounded ominous:

Hi Julian,

I called the vet this evening and she explained the results
of Valerie's blood tests. There are some abnormalities with
her kidneys, there are increased kidney enzymes and she is
slightly anaemic, which could be related to the kidney disease.

She would like to discuss with you further, regarding treatment. She will be on duty at the surgery tomorrow up to
12.30 p.m.

Please be assured, Julian, I'm taking care of Valerie and
she is nice and cosy and comfy here. As I type she is curled
up next to me on your sofa, snoring!!!

Hermione

The next day, when I spoke to the vet – the same one who had
witnessed my hysteria – I could tell she was treading carefully
around the subject of end-of-life care for Valerie, no doubt wary
of setting me off again. But I knew what was coming. Valerie was
fading away and if grim decisions had to be made I must make
them with a level head and not make it more upsetting than it
already was.

I had a few days off from touring, followed by dates in Folkestone and Canterbury. Valerie was terribly sick and listless: I had to carry her out to the garden and up to bed, where I spent the night listening to her rasping breathing and moans. This was only heading in one direction, and I decided to spare her any more suffering and arranged for the vet to come at 2 p.m. the next afternoon.

I spent the morning with Valerie, stroking her and telling her what a perfect, beautiful dog she had been. She occasionally looked at me with watery eyes, but mostly she slept. Hermione kept Albert occupied. He came and looked at Valerie once or twice. Who knows what one dog senses about another, what level of communication they have?

The vet was solemn, kind and gentle. She had a nurse with her who I suspected might be there more for my benefit, just in case. Valerie was asleep in her favourite place in the sun and didn't wake up while the vet gave her the injection. I sat next door in the window seat, looking out at the sky. The vet came in. 'It's all done,' she said, and asked if I'd like to see Valerie. I looked into the room and saw Valerie, just as she had been five minutes before, but I didn't go closer. I didn't wish to see her final stillness. I sent Albert in instead but he didn't stay long. Valerie was wrapped in a towel and carried respectfully out to the car.

CHAPTER 21

Further Developments

I found a jaunty wooden box for Valerie's ashes and, ever since, have kept them next to Fanny's. It is the box I used to keep my drugs in, back in the day, and since she had given me as much pleasure as they did, it seems appropriate. There they sit, sentry-like, my dead daughters in repose. I imagine them both in their prime, watching my every move. In death they are endowed with more human qualities and can speak and discuss things, both with each other and me, which is an unexpected boon. Fanny is the more playful of the two, her remarks facetious and witty, while Valerie tuts and worries. Fanny nods approvingly at the third glass of sauvignon blanc while Valerie raises an eyebrow and urges caution. The marvellous news about death – and this extends to everyone – is that the love never dies and therefore neither does the host. I may start a religious sect with this truth one day. My followers and I will live happily on an isolated hilltop somewhere, smoking opium and communing with the dear departed. We will wear only sparkly Lycra and we will have rotas for everything, like cleaning the toilets and preparing the sushi, from which I, as leader, will be exempt.

Having a dog put to sleep is an act of kindness. Or it should be. I have an acquaintance who had an elderly dog who was fine, just a bit old and slow. I saw him one winter morning in early January and he was alone.

'Where's the dog?' I asked.

'You know what, girlfriend?' he said, rolling his eyes. 'I thought new year, new beginning. I need to shed some kilos.'

He'd had his dog put to sleep because she was interfering with his resolution to be more active.

Someone I knew in Kent had two Jack Russell bitches. When one died the other one missed her friend, which was upsetting to witness. 'So I took her outside and shot her,' he told me. Makes you wonder how he would treat his elderly relatives when they had outlived their usefulness.

Speaking of which, I'm fairly sure my parents have a secret pact not to be any 'trouble' to their children. Over the last few years they have had the odd fall, aneurism or broken bone, a spot of breast cancer or fluid around the heart. All were dealt with briskly, with no demands for concern or sympathy. They were soon back on their feet. Now they were well into their eighties and the 'everything is fine and always will be' act was less convincing.

I knew my father had a hospital appointment about something sinister going on in his lungs. Much to their amusement, I decided I ought to take him.

'But I can catch the bus!' said my father. 'I get on it over the bridge by the swings and it takes me right to the door. And you don't have to pay for parking that way.'

'I'd go,' said my mother, 'but I've got a bowls match on.'

Perhaps they were in denial – which I'm all for, as it happens – but I took him nevertheless.

The doctor began by showing us the CT scan of my father's lungs and the 'suspicious' mass and the honeycomb bubbles which are the features of chronic obstructive pulmonary disease (COPD). Treatment at his age, she said, was limited to what his body could cope with. 'But we'll make sure that you're comfortable. . .' she said significantly.

A diagnostic bronchoscopy was the next stage.

Back home my mother said, 'Your father can be a bit negative sometimes. He told me yesterday that I wouldn't be able to have the hanging baskets next year as the watering can is too heavy for me.'

They still walked their dog Suzi each day, but it was more of a slow meander than a vigorous romp.

In cheerier news, on 19 November 2016, Rolf slipped his finger into my ring at last. His main concern, when he insisted I marry him, was that he would be perceived as a gold-digger. I said, 'Rolf [or 'Melania' as he prefers to be called], don't be silly.'

The only thing that calmed him down was the gift of a new Cartier watch.

Then there's the age difference between us – seventeen years – which is, in my opinion, nothing short of scandalous. Rolf, I know, has come to terms with this. Why else would his wedding day card to me have included a laminated card with the contact details for Dignitas and a one-way ticket to Switzerland?

Our wedding day was a nice day out and terribly exclusive – just us and two witnesses at Camden Town Hall. We didn't want any fuss. As the registrar said, it was so intimate, we could have got married in a toilet cubicle. I said, 'It's funny you should say that. That's exactly where we met'. A joke, of course, but it didn't go well. A big, fancy wedding would never have worked for us. Picture the scene: my elegant, well-bred family and celebrity chums attempting to mix and mingle with a coachload of Geordies demanding gravy with their sushi and saying 'What's this shit?' when offered a glass of vintage champagne.

But the happy day was also Rolf's fortieth birthday, so we had arranged a big party that evening. We hung a 'Just Married!' sign over the front door so that guests knew, and much ooh-ing and aah-ing ensued.

Curiously, it had been the horrific Bataclan Theatre massacre in Paris on 13 November 2015 that led to our marriage. Seeing so many lives ended so suddenly and senselessly made us contemplate our own lives. We felt the need to get our affairs in order. We made our wills, then one thing led to another. I didn't get down on one knee – not at my age. Thanks to the determined and heroic efforts of LGBT human rights crusaders, queer relationships were now considered as worthy of legal status as the quaint heterosexual variety and we could, if we wished, have the same benefits and protections. Civil partnerships had graciously been permitted for a while, but – call me a lapsed Catholic – I wanted the real thing. God forbid anything should happen to either of us, but if it did we wanted to be assured that the other would be okay. I'd sung a song about this on stage called 'Cool to be Queer'.

> *We're legal now and yes, we're fit to wed,*
> *And we ain't sinners, Desmond Tutu said.*

Now it was time to take the plunge ourselves and make our solemn vows. Fidelity can be a sticking point for the gays, but we're giving it a go – and I speak as one who used to think that monogamy was just a board game. Should things go tits up, Rolf has what he calls his 'List for Fiona Shackleton', where he carefully records all my misdemeanours for the celebrity divorce lawyer.

'Fiona shall hear of this!' he cries if I break wind or burn the toast.

Luckily for Rolf, I am possessed by a variety of different spirits and he can never be sure just who is going to enter the bridal chamber. Last night I was 'Odette', a highly aroused, insatiable non-binary French minx who breathes saucy suggestions in their native tongue and sometimes does unspeakable things with the bedside torch. Less seductive is 'Geoffrey', a cardigan-wearing old codger who lives in a bungalow in Essex and suffers from blocked sinuses, but he still enjoys an imaginative love life and gives detailed, interminable accounts of his dogging expeditions at motorway service stations. 'There was a memorable occasion at Clacket Lane in the summer of 1976. . .'.

I like being married, and refer to 'my husband' at every possible opportunity. The novelty never seems to wear off. Rolf makes me tea every morning before he rushes off to his mysterious place of work, and if I'm not too busy being theatrical I make sure he has something hot on the table when he gets home. Then we have dinner. It's a comfort to know I'm no longer on the shelf, gathering dust like Anthea Turner's autobiography. Marriage is a hoot, and if you're living somewhere that doesn't allow pets, I highly recommend it. Rolf tells me that business is booming and I've every reason to hope that, when the time comes, my home care package will be top of the range.

Meanwhile, I try to remain faithful, but it isn't easy. He will keep going out of the room.

The day after our nuptials, I started rehearsals for *Cinderella*. Panto was returning to the London Palladium for the first time in thirty years, and I was to share the stage with Paul O'Grady. As I settled into the same dressing room that Judy Garland, Liberace, Marie Lloyd and Bruce Forsyth (among others) had occupied, I thought of Valerie and Fanny and how much they deserved to be sitting there with me. The next day I brought in the two boxes and placed them on my make-up table.

'There you are, girls,' I said. 'Where you belong.'

In all the decades I had known Savage, we had never performed together. This was probably just as well, as we had a lot of trouble getting through one scene without giggling like a couple of schoolgirls. The difficulty started in rehearsals and went on and on throughout the five-week run, despite doing the show twelve times a week. It just never stopped. Savage was playing the evil Baroness von Savage and I was Dandini. There was one scene in the woods, where our conversation was interrupted by a curious smell, which I assumed was caused by the Baroness from her time spent at Battersea Dogs Home.

BARONESS: The whiff is coming from your direction.
DANDINI: Ah. That'll be my muff.
BARONESS: That old thing has seen some wear.
DANDINI. Yes, look at it. Completely stretched out of shape.
BARONESS: You could get the seven dwarves in there.
DANDINI: I've only ever managed five. . .[12]

Such nonsense wasn't to everyone's taste, alas, as this letter post-marked from Medway informed me:

Clary
   We took our family to see THE PANTO and were disgusted by your filthy references to homosexual 'JOKES'?
   You upset many, many familys [sic] and children.
   Hope your [sic] proud of yourself.
   Look in the mirror with all the lightbulbs around it and what do you see?
   A SICK PERVERT WHO COULDN'T CARE LESS

I showed the letter to our director, who said, 'You must tell your mother to stop writing to you at the theatre.'

It's a shame when someone who has paid for a ticket doesn't enjoy my performance but when they clearly have problems (poor grammar and spelling being the tip of the iceberg here), I can't help but be secretly thrilled. And, as we shall see, it didn't stop them coming again the following year. And the next. There's nowt so queer as folk.

Meanwhile, my parents' dog, Suzi from Glasgow with the pendulous breasts, had died of cancer. I had assumed that my parents were of an age when they wouldn't consider another dog. But making assumptions is never a good idea. A few years earlier I'd been walking the dogs with my father and thought it might be reassuring for him to know I'd look after Suzi if necessary in the future. Given the recent diagnosis of his terminal respiratory condition, it seemed a sensible suggestion.

'What do you mean?' he asked, frowning at me.

'Just that, if anything happens I'll take care of Suzi.'

'What might happen? I don't understand.'

'I thought you might worry sometimes about the dog. Should you . . .'.

'What? I don't understand what you're saying.'

I didn't pursue the conversation.

So, within days of Suzi's death, my father was talking about getting another. My suggestion that he look at the Oldies website and find a nice, lazy mature dog didn't go down well.

'No, thank you. I'd like the fun of a puppy. I don't want an old dog that's going to die on me, thank you very much.'

As it happened, Amanda Holden was playing the fairy godmother in *Cinderella* and was talking excitedly over lunch (five grapes in a Tupperware box for her, a generous tuna baguette with chips on the side for me) about the new puppy that she was getting the next week. It was a 'designer' dog – a cross between a Bichon Frise and a Shih Tzu (the same as Savage's Buster, as it happens). 'No moulting and a very easy-going temperament,' she informed me. She showed me photos of her puppy on her phone: an adorable bundle of white and pale grey fur. Looked ideal for my father, and as luck would have it there was another pup available. My father agreed, so Whiskey was his Christmas present. I presented Whiskey to him in my dressing room at the Palladium after my parents came to see the show. I know I said previously that one must choose one's own puppy by psychic means, but my father's need was urgent – so what was good enough for Amanda Holden would have to be good enough for him.

A puppy living with a couple in their mid-eighties is a good idea for a sitcom. Much hilarity ensued. Whiskey's idea of fun was to steal a pair of knickers and run around the house and garden with them for a couple of hours, pursued by two breathless pensioners.

My old friend Nick, meanwhile, was also busy – he was racking up the requisite number of hours counselling people he needed to gain the certification required to set up in practice as a psychotherapist. He'd experienced some difficulty swallowing recently, and a sinister growth had been revealed behind his tonsils. When we'd last met for a lunch of kedgeree and lemon mousse he'd looked unwell, and I did my utmost to dismiss my worries. He emailed me the following week.

I was up at the crack on Saturday to go for a PET scan at UCLH, thereafter beguiled the hours reading E.H.

Young's *Miss Mole*, watching Barbara Stanwyck in *Stella Dallas*, listening to the opera, having a L'Oréal face pack and making chicken noodle soup.

Yesterday I assessed a patient who is having pathological intrusive thoughts about death since her stepfather succumbed to cancer, and we discussed the reluctance to reflect on death, despite it being the one thing in life we are guaranteed. Always cheerful, me.

I wondered if he was trying to tell me something.

CHAPTER 22

A Big Decision

What with ageing parents and Nick's health to worry about, I had a lot on my mind. As usual, I tried to distract myself with work. A couple of what might be called 'highbrow' projects came my way next. Sky Arts had a series called Passions and I was invited to present a documentary about Noël Coward, investigating his life – his birth in Teddington, his career, his years in Kent and then in Jamaica, where he died. The idea was to get to know the 'real' Noël behind the carefully constructed façade. I visited his grave at Firefly and scattered some rose petals from the garden at Goldenhurst there. It was rather wonderful.

I was bringing Coward's country home back to life, so to be paid to find out more about him, and to then spend that dosh on his house, felt like something he would have approved of. I had to be respectful. I had to get it right, or the ghosts would let me know. And there was so much history to look into: the parties, the visitors, the war years – it was all there in his diaries, letters and biographies. I had his whole life, not to mention his extensive work (songs, plays, poems, short stories and more) to investigate, and I like to think I have an idea about what he was like as a man. At Goldenhurst, with a little imagination I could feel his presence, sense his disapproval or enthusiasm, hear him muttering over my shoulder. He made me smile almost every day.

The more I discovered in the making of the programme, the more I warmed to the real, private Noël. I think he knew that laughter is a great healer, and he used his wit kindly. Most of the time.

He was elusive, in the sense that he wasn't here to sit down and have cheery private chats with, but being able to converse with those who knew him and to visit the places he went to, that he loved, and the spot where he is buried, I got a little closer to the man himself.

He had dogs, too – a black poodle called Charlie and two dachshunds apparently called 'the Camaroons'. Another poodle of his, called Matelot, attempted to rape the vicar when he visited, according to Noël's diaries: 'I removed him, saying, "Matelot, not the vicar!"'

There are some scratch marks on the upstairs bathroom door that look suspiciously as if they are of canine origin. . .

It is a strange thing to contemplate someone who is dead and gone, but I wonder, would he like me? Would he approve? Am I too much? Too vulgar? Are the soft furnishings to Noël's taste? The curtains? The pictures on the walls? The colour of the roses? These are questions that can never be answered. But we can try.

I think Noël Coward knew that life was sometimes harsh, tough and dull. In his plays and performances it never was, though, and he did his best to live a life that was elegant and charming and sparkling. He knew the need for escapism. Perhaps he can teach us from the grave how to do the same.

After I finished filming the Coward documentary, I acted in a play called *Le Grand Mort* at the Trafalgar Studios, which had been written for me by the late Steven Clark. There were an awful lot of words to learn – a twenty-minute monologue to start things off, which I had to deliver while cooking pasta alla puttanesca, if you please.

'Steven Clark's puzzling drama about a man planning to either seduce or murder his dinner guest comes across as both morbid and exploitative,' sniffed Michael Billington from the *Guardian*.[13] Maybe. The same reviewer called my performance in *Cinderella* 'a tsunami of smut' – one of my favourite press cuttings ever.

Acting is a different world from being a comedy turn, as I found out. I'm so used to speaking directly to the audience – who at the Trafalgar Studios are just inches away from the performers – that it was second nature to me to enhance the script with a few withering remarks about the front row's choice of footwear on the opening night. I got some laughs and was pleased with myself – but the director, Chris Renshaw, was less so. It seems my improvisations might have spoilt the magic of the moment and turned a carefully crafted play into the Julian Clary Show. It wasn't about me; it was about the author's vision. This was a learning curve if ever there was one. I taught myself to ignore the audience – even if they decided to leave halfway through by walking across the stage to get to the exit – when I just wanted to give them what for. In the course of the play my co-star, a fine actor called James Nelson-Joyce, was required to take off all his clothes and throw me about. Word of his fine physique and generous endowment reached the dirty raincoat brigade, and I had to turn a blind eye to the odd spot of furtive self-pleasuring, for which I deserve an award, in my humble opinion.

I was back in more familiar territory by Christmas, with a return to panto at the Palladium. Our second season was *Dick Whittington*. I was an ethereal being called the Spirit of the Bells and I got to duet with Elaine Paige, who was Queen Rat. ('For another fiver we could have had Marti Webb'.) We bastardised an Andrew Lloyd Webber song and sang 'We Know Dick So Well'.

For a camp old turn like me, this was all too thrilling. I had to pinch myself every day to make sure I wasn't dreaming. I was knocking sixty and if you'd told me I would have been lucky to be working in the back room of the Three Cocky Sailors, I wouldn't have quibbled. It was my good fortune that Michael Harrison at Qdos had a taste for smut and the good sense to team me up with Gary Wilmot, Paul Zerdin, and, er, Nigel Havers. The set, the costumes, the choreography, the band, the dancers – everything was top-notch.

Although I thanked my lucky stars that I was in such company, all sorts of things went through my mind each day as I waited for my first entrance. I was suspended on a giant swing high above the stage, ready to be lowered in for my opening number, 'You Can Ring My Bell'. I'd be swaying from side to side between the flats and lights, listening to Nigel Havers milk the scene far below, sure I was about to plunge to my doom, my knees buckling with terror.

Before any show, wherever I am, I always imagine that there's a circular gap in the sky just above me where departed friends and relatives look down on me, wishing me well. It is a different selection each night, although Steven, bless him, rarely misses a show, even if I have the misfortune to be playing in Chatham. Sometimes my grandparents are there, Auntie Tess, Christopher, Fanny and Valerie. Since this was the Palladium, there was always a good turnout, but also lots of faces that I didn't recognise but which were faintly familiar. I knew these were distant relatives who shared my sense of humour and who were kind and benevolent. There too, on occasion, are my old friends from my Edinburgh Festival days, Russell Churney and Michael Parker. I realise that these fanciful visions are a result of a Catholic upbringing, but the comfort they bring, the fluffiness of the clouds and the beatific smiles from the heavenly dead are so real to me that I choose to open up my spirit to them. It's better than suffering stage fright. I'll say no more. *Dick Whittington* won an Olivier.

The only tricky thing in all this was Albert. Having set up a blissful domestic situation at Goldenhurst, with the house and garden as grand and comfortable as I could make it and Hermione there to tend to our every need, we found ourselves living and working in London. I could hardly leave Hermione there in solitary confinement in the middle of nowhere in the dead of winter, so Albert stayed with her. We missed him terribly. Life without a dog is miserable. I dashed down there on my one day off each week, and Hermione served me Jersey Royals and poured me gin, and referred to Albert as 'my partner in crime', but the whole arrangement seemed unsatisfactory, off-centre. I felt guilty about being separated from Albert and guilty about Hermione's lack of anyone (human) to look after. But at least I felt sure that the house was safe and ticking over. It needed to be prodded and petted. It wasn't the sort of place you could leave unattended. It was too demanding, too temperamental.

It's hard to describe how brain-dead you feel during panto season. Or maybe I'm just speaking for myself. Not on stage, as far as I'm aware, but off. I think it's my way of preserving energy. The show takes over every corner of my brain and there is no room for anything else. Even when asleep I swear the show is running on a loop in my head.

'You're only on stage for a couple of hours!' my father scoffed as I sat with glassy eyes over Christmas lunch.

So as soon as the curtain comes down on the last performance I'm poured into a taxi and taken to the airport to catch a plane to somewhere sunny. For the first few days I sit in silence, much to Rolf's relief, on a sun lounger, slowly reclaiming my thoughts. It's generally mid-March before I say or do or think anything interesting.

As well as doing panto, I was also writing The Bolds, my series of children's books. There are six so far – I knock one out most summers – and they are my secret delight. I regress to being a child when I'm writing them, and it is more therapy than toil. But there's no point in writing a book if people don't know about it, so twice a year, to announce the hardback and paperback publication, I set to the job of publicising. The publicist for Andersen Press, which publishes my children's books, is, shall we say, keen. His motto is 'No journey too long, no event too small'. He's very pleasant. One of those stocky, bearded gay men who wears tight *Love Island* trousers and shows you photos of the Afghan cushions his 'other half' bought for their love nest in Dulwich. His favourite word is 'really', which he pronounces 'rarely', on account of coming from Hull. It's always 'rarely, rarely important' that I schlep to some shithole in the provinces as a matter of urgency. Luckily for him, he has charm and a steely determination to sell books, so I do anything he asks, as long as he gets me a warm almond croissant (if I have an early start) or a gin and tonic for the train journey home.

So to 'celebrate' *The Bolds Go Wild* I found myself, often with my illustrator, the talented David Roberts, attending Chiswick Book Festival, the *Zoe Ball On Saturday* TV show, Bath Festival, Hay Festival, Cheltenham Festival, the Attitude Awards, *This Morning*, South Bank Children's Festival, the Independent Booksellers Awards, Michael Ball's Radio 2 show, school events in Bishop's Stortford, Teddington, Leeds and Manchester, a Kensington Library book event, and a tour of independent bookshops in north London.

Sometimes there is a token payment for your trouble, but the understanding is you do it for the book sales – although after the event in Hay, I was presented with a paper rose made from cleverly folded newspaper. Something to treasure.

You have to get your laughs where you can. During the Q&A session after a presentation in a primary school in Leeds I moved among the audience with the microphone, keen to make sure that everyone got to ask their question.

'I'm just going up the back, if you'll pardon the expression.' I say this sort of thing for the amusement of any teachers present, you understand. I'm not expecting knowing laughs from primary school kids.

'If you could be any animal, what would you be?' asked a little girl.

'I'd like to be a crab playing on the seashore,' replied David the illustrator dreamily.

'That's nice,' I said. 'Do you have much experience of crabs?'

His attempts not to laugh turned David's lips into a perfect cat's bottom.

Thirty minutes after the signing in Edinburgh I was on the train back to London, reading *Queer City – Gay London from the Romans to the Present Day* by Peter Ackroyd. The hours flew by as I read with interest: 'The "camp" comedian . . . is almost as old as London itself. A gay harlequinade was staged as early as 1702, when the Mard Brothers performed a "night piece".' This gave me a warm glow. My place in the subculture of London is pre-destined. I'm not a tired old queen after all, I thought, yawning.

It was gone 10 p.m. by the time I got home to Camden, and the husband was asleep. Albert managed a wag of the tail but that was the extent of my greeting. I put my case on the bed to unpack it, then shrieked when I opened it and realised it wasn't my case at all, but one remarkably similar. The husband wasn't best pleased, as I woke him up and he had to remove his earplugs.

The rogue case was neatly packed with what I judged to be 'gay' clothes – low range designer and fastidiously, symmetrically packed. The toiletries bag was crammed with drugs for every occasion, from Temazepam to other more recreational powders and potions. There was an Australian passport in the front pocket. The bag belonged to a man I'll call Donald Marsden, aged thirty. He was quite dishy, in a dilated-pupil sort of way. I googled 'King's Cross lost property' but there was no phone number to call, just a dreary contact form to fill in.

'What if Donald is on his way to Heathrow for his flight back to Perth?' I asked.

The husband had a brainwave and went on Facebook. He found Donald on there, left him a message and within seconds got a call from him. Donald had my bag and was wandering around King's Cross, distraught. So the husband got dressed and drove me to the station, where we furtively swapped our bags outside the Five Guys burger bar. The CCTV camera on the lamp post swivelled round to catch the transaction.

Half an hour later the drama was over and we were back home. The husband returned to bed and I unpacked my own case. Take two. I thought it would be a wonder if I could sleep after all the excitement, so I slipped one of Donald's Temazepam under my tongue. I'm sure he'd understand. Albert was snoring heavily.

Some of the TV 'ideas' that came my way were of the 'so bad they might be good' variety. *It's Behind You!* was sold to me as a new Saturday night show for BBC1. The concept was this: a number of punters stand holding a pyramid of champagne glasses. They must hold their nerve while various things happen behind them that might cause them to spill the drinks: a huge balloon is burst, an opera singer hits a top C. The winner is the person with the most upright glasses left at the end. They win a holiday on the Isle of Wight. We workshopped the show in a church hall and the commissioning editor came to watch. She agreed with my assessment: crap.

Another proposal was called *My Big Gay House*. Initially this was to be me driving around America with a minibus full of LGBT pensioners investigating alternative care homes. The budget was then cut and the show was re-presented to me as six international LGBT pensioners coming to live with me at Goldenhurst. As if I wanted some incontinent old lesbian from Baltimore weeing on my carpet. I'd rather do a remake of the test card. I politely declined and the show was offered to Sue Perkins before sinking without trace.

Sadly, the one show I would dearly love to do on TV is already taken. *Love Your Garden*. Since it's a garden show, Albert could come with me, I reasoned. The format requires a punter who is either terminally ill or recently bereaved. They are then lured away from their modest home on some flimsy pretext while Alan Titchmarsh and his team sneak into their garden. In a trice they rip everything out, install the cheapest water feature they can find, plant some half-dead shrubs and, if there's time, sprinkle some awful coloured gravel around. The recently bereaved then return to their home and are shown the vandalised garden, and inevitably they cry. I love it. If only Alan would do the decent thing and retire, then my dream could come true. Sigh.

Mind you, one of the exciting things about showbiz is that you never know what might be around the corner. One day my agent called me and, sounding rather bemused, told me that a very famous film director had asked to meet me. I'd been summoned. I was all of a flutter, as you can imagine. I turned up at the appointed hour at the swanky production office just off Oxford Street and was shown into a hot glass booth with harsh sunshine beaming through a large window. The director was there, affable in baggy jeans. He had a youthful, rather ruthless-looking assistant with him who scrutinised me during the small talk.

'You should be in films,' said the director, as if I'd been withholding my services to the industry.

'That would be nice,' I replied weakly. I sounded a bit like Quentin Crisp, for some reason.

'Why haven't you?' asked his assistant accusingly.

'I did *Carry on Camping*,' I offered.

'What sort of film would you like to make?' asked the director.

'Er,' I fumbled. 'Comedy?' Then I worried that I'd said the wrong thing. 'On the other hand, something serious might be good.'

There was a gentle snort from the assistant.

Then the director told a story about a dinner party he'd been to recently with Sophia Loren. Sophia told him she had once been introduced to Mae West. As she leant in to kiss Mae on the cheek, the director said, 'She knew at that moment that Mae West was a man.'

'Really?' I said. *Where was all this going?* 'Are you asking me to play the part of Mae West?'

'Why not?' said the director without blinking.

My mind was racing. It seemed unlikely casting, but I was already imagining myself in my trailer after several hours in prosthetics. I'd need a vocal coach. But the film would be a huge hit and my dwindling career would suddenly soar in a new, surprising direction. I'd probably have to move to Hollywood.

What about the dog? He couldn't travel in the hold. I'd need a private jet.

'I'm doing a tour next spring,' I said, getting quite carried away with the idea. 'I'm free after June, though.' As soon as the words left my mouth, I realised I was jumping the gun to an Olympic degree. There was an awkward pause and the assistant's expression turned ever so slightly minty. There was a bit more chat about the books I've written, but the director's eyes had lost their twinkle and his assistant's jaw was beginning to twitch.

'Anyway, I just thought it would be interesting to meet you,' the director said, standing up. 'I'm a big fan.'

His assistant held the door open for me and nodded in the direction of the lifts.

There comes a time in every camp comic's career that panto, touring and knocking out the odd book seem like very attractive prospects: you do the graft, earn a crust and maintain your dignity. Self-sufficiency. Really, it's all I ever wanted from life.

That's when the idea of selling Goldenhurst popped into my mind. I was horrified. I'd spent the last twelve years bringing the place up to scratch. I'd spent a small fortune on it. It was perfect now. I loved it. How could I bear to part with it? But the thought sat stubbornly in my head, pulsating like a strange sea creature risen from the depths. *You need to sell Goldenhurst. Move on.* I hoped the thought would go away, but it didn't. Maybe the communication was coming from the house itself? It was starting to play its old tricks again: doors would jam shut. The lights would flicker and go out. The chimney became mysteriously blocked. One day I was walking across the front lawn towards the house with Albert when I heard a strange creaking sound: an organic, earthy scream. I turned around just in time to see a massive branch fall off the elm tree. It landed with a thud just a few feet from where I was standing, paralysed and disorientated. It bounced, and leaves flew up in the air around it like a flock of sinister birds. Albert ran to the kitchen door, staring back at the lawn. If the branch had fallen a few seconds earlier or I had walked a little slower, I would be dead. It took the gardener and the odd-job man several days to chop up the fallen branch with a chainsaw. The now lopsided elm stood there accusingly, the raw, white wound of the torn limb on display, as if I was responsible for its ugly new disability.

I tried to think things through rationally, making lists of the pros and cons.

Reasons to stay

- I had poured my heart and soul into Goldenhurst, done all manner of jobs to earn the money to spend on its refurbishments.
- All the major expenses were done with now. It was as I wanted it.
- It was my haven, my escape from the stress and strains of London. It made me very happy.
- It was a valuable asset.
- I could, as I'd always imagined, spend my old age there, pottering about in a state of rustic bliss.

- It gave me space to breathe and entertain.
- What about Maureen?
- Albert loved the garden and Valerie had enjoyed her best years at Goldenhurst.
- What would I do with all the stuff if I left? Furniture, books and art?
- I loved it.

Reasons to sell

- The voice in my head.
- Staying meant that my life was all mapped out, and that was boring. I could simplify my life and prepare for another adventure, as yet unknown.
- It might be more fun to live in central London as I got older.
- Really, it was too big for me.
- There was bound to be more expense, sooner or later.
- Valerie was gone. Every time I stepped into the garden I thought of her, and that made me a little sad. Walking Albert in the Kent countryside was lovely, but we hardly ever met another dog walker and Albert wasn't socialising with other dogs. He loved Regent's Park and had lots of friends there.
- Rolf worked in London and could only come to Goldenhurst at weekends.
- Sometimes you have to let go of the things you love.

In the end I heeded the voice. It wasn't unkind in any way. It wasn't urging me to self-harm. In fact, it seemed wise and reasonable. Maybe it knew something I didn't. In fact, I realised, it was much like the voice that had told me to get a dog at the age of twenty-one, so it wasn't to be ignored. The reasons would become clear later. For all I knew, there might be a global pandemic around the corner and all sources of my income would disappear. I decided to trust the inner voice.

I didn't tell anyone apart from my husband about my decision. The estate agent was sworn to secrecy and the property wasn't to be advertised – she would whip the details out from under the table when she judged a suitable buyer might be looking in the vicinity. Having done photo shoots, interviews, books and TV programmes about Goldenhurst, I imagined that people might be surprised, if not suspicious, about why I was selling. They might wonder, with relish, whether I'd fallen upon hard times. It wasn't for me to tell them that I had heard freedom calling me and I was obeying, like a lost dog in the woods.

I also thought this would be a good time to reclaim my privacy. Since I had told the world where I lived, it was not unusual for people to come and knock on the door if they were overcome by the urge to see a camp comic in the flesh. A car once screeched to a halt when I was in the front garden picking gooseberries and a woman leapt out and started taking photos of me on her smartphone. I'd hazard a guess she was from Ashford.

'There he is!' she cried triumphantly. 'Where's the other one?'

She meant Paul O'Grady. *The other one.* I try not to be rude to the general public, but there are occasions when I let them have it.

I decided to be more circumspect in future about my whereabouts. I'd reclaim my celebrity mystique.

Wasn't that former celebrity Julian Whatshisname I just glimpsed on the beach at Hunstanton wearing a balaclava? No, it can't be!

The day dawned. It was a perfect June morning, with the sun shining in a cloudless sky, Maureen scratching happily on the freshly mown lawn, roses cascading everywhere. I opened all the windows and lit some incense. Hermione was busy baking bread in the kitchen and I sat decoratively at my desk, beautifully lit by flattering sunlight, Albert asleep by my side. A person of note was coming to view the house and I knew – just knew – before he arrived that he would buy it.

'I'm interested. Very interested,' he said meaningfully. Well, why wouldn't he be? That was more or less that. Solicitors were engaged and there was some distasteful correspondence about where exactly my sewage went, as the house wasn't connected to mains drainage and had no septic tank. It wasn't a conundrum that had occupied my mind till now. A man was sent with a camera, if you please, to poke along pipes and solve the mystery. 'Nice work if you can get it', I said to him. The answer – for those who feel the need to know, was something to do with the nether regions of a nearby field. I believe I glazed over when this gripping information was imparted.

Hermione said a tearful goodbye and I set about clearing the house of everything I had acquired. The hospice shop furniture returned to its source and I sold, donated, gifted or placed other items in storage. It was all very cleansing. Somewhere in Ramsgate is a storage facility with all my rustic essentials in it – the Queen Anne bed, rugs, crockery, cutlery, paintings and dog bowls. One day, the plan is, I shall find another nook in the countryside and start again. Or else it will stay there, a time capsule gathering dust for some distant relative to sort through. God bless beautiful Kent. I shall visit from time to time, and I feel a surge of affection whenever I look at photos from my time at Goldenhurst. But I have passed the baton to someone else.

So it was back to Camden, where happiness reigns and there are BLM posters in the windows, not BNP posters.

CHAPTER 23

Camden Capers

Now, as I write about the more recent past, I am swimming towards my present self in ever shallower waters. What happens when I get to my destination? Perhaps that's when the book becomes a diary – or, if I go further, a sort of science-fiction fantasy of my future. That could be fun. 'Suddenly, at the age of seventy, my career hit its long-awaited peak . . . I was living in a luxurious penthouse with my second husband, Jamie Dornan, who would *not* leave me alone. . .'.

I haven't had time to make sense of things, to gestate them from now on, so you must bear with me, as they say at call centres. It's far more chic to leave the party with a sense of things withheld but I can't, as there is another dog on the horizon. We must bite the pillow and press fearlessly onwards.

During this time, Nick's health continued to deteriorate, although his emails were funny and never self-pitying.

Went to the Ear, Nose and Throat Hospital this a.m. to meet my anaesthetist, a lovely Asian man. He had me walk up and down two flights of stairs with him, while chatting, to form an idea of my stamina. I hadn't realised what a big deal it is being out for the count via a fusion of specially blended gases, considering how frequently I used to do it myself with nothing more than a litre of Tanqueray gin.

The information sheet about the anaesthetic says that I've not to do the ironing, sign legal documents or lift children afterwards . . . Apropos the op, I mustn't blow my nose for two weeks, and avoid sneezing.

Salmon salad makes my mouth water for its deliciousness, but my blood runs cold at the painful crunchiness. The cream for my caramel turned while it was heating, but I wasn't inspired by the recipe, so bugger Delia Smith, am starting again with a BBC Good Food simple one. Plus having a craze on banana milk and Weetabix hooshmied up in creamy coffee, gourmet that I am. Also liking the morphine, which enables me to continue chewing and swallowing – a few more pushes of the syringe and I'll be sticking a gardenia in my hair and singing like my shoes are too tight.

It's tedious, though, being a doctor's delight. I am under the care of an oncologist, a hepatologist, a maxillo-facial specialist, a dietician, a special needs dentist and a speech and language therapist, so apart from the cancer and a burgeoning dependency on morphine, I'm as fit as a butcher's dog!

In 2018 my parents celebrated their sixty-fifth wedding anniversary with a large family gathering in a hotel in Swindon. The restaurant was next to the spa so there was a distinct whiff of chlorine and (I suspect) Lynx in the air. Not unpleasant. I took photos of my parents to compare to the wedding album they had brought with them. From youth to old age, there they were, and here they are still. A week earlier, my mother had given me a copy of Julian Barnes' *The Only Story*. It is about love and life and is rather wonderful: 'Which was the correct – or the more correct – formulation: "Life is beautiful but sad" or "Life is sad but beautiful?"'

A few weeks earlier, I had taken my mother to the Chelsea Flower Show. It was the press day, which means that celebs of almost any rank are invited. We can wander around without being jostled by civilians, with their constant demand for selfies. But of course there is no such thing as a free peony: the general public were replaced by journalists – similar to the general public but with cheaper jewellery. They're everywhere, like greenfly. We come to Chelsea most years. The year before we were walking along admiring the lupin display and chatting about my grandfather's garden in Norfolk when I realised my mother was no longer beside me. I looked around to see her legs sticking out of a flower bed. So that morning I presented her with a walking stick: a posh one I found in Trumper's of Marylebone with a silver handle and a carving of a cat on the shaft. She wasn't keen, but used it to please me.

Everywhere you look there are people you know, so there's a lot of smiling and nodding. In the distance I saw Piers Morgan striding confidently along. Interesting to note that when people saw him they suddenly took an interest in the garden in the other direction. It was like a herd of gazelles suddenly becoming aware of a hyena in their midst and veering off in the interests of self-preservation.

Inevitably we bumped into Nigel Havers and his wife. They are clearly very much in love. Nigel was appropriately dressed in a blue blazer and a cream Panama. His wife, George, looked a little pink around the gills. I suspect they'd had a heavy petting session in the taxi on the way to Chelsea. Or behind the tea tent. I shook his hand then sniffed my fingers: just as I thought.

An awful woman from the *Daily Mail* waylaid us, her chewed pencil hovering over a notebook. She was quite worked up because an A-list celebrity had just been 'extremely rude' to her, she said. I sensed danger. She was looking for revenge.

'Do you like him?' she asked me.

I said I don't know him very well.

'Do you think he's got any talent?'

'He's very popular,' I said.

She huffed with frustration. 'Oh, loosen up!' she barked, then turned to my mother. Had she seen the Jeremy Thorpe 'thing', *A Very English Scandal*, on TV the other night?

Yes.

'What about all that sex? Wasn't it disgusting? So rough!'

'Well. . .' My mother shrugged, stroking the shaft of her walking stick. 'It's like that sometimes, isn't it?'

In 2018 more shameless filth was called for in *Snow White* at the Palladium, where I had the great pleasure of performing as the Man in the Mirror with Dawn French as Queen Dragonella. Dawn is very down to earth – some might say common. She doesn't kick off as long as she gets her Cornish pasty delivered from Greggs at lunchtime. Being from Cornwall, she takes her make-up off with clotted cream, so there's a faint whiff of dairy produce about her. But apart from that I have no complaints.

DRAGONELLA: Flatter me properly and I'll reward you with a Terry's chocolate orange.

JC: If it's all the same to you, I'd rather have a Terry's chocolate finger.

DRAGONELLA: Mirror, mirror on the wall, who is the fairest of them all?

JC: Except I'm not on the wall, am I? I haven't been up against a wall since my night out with Harry Styles. Talk about One Direction. . .[14]

And, of course, it isn't a Palladium panto without Nigel Havers.

NIGEL: This year I'm the keeper of the Royal Orchard.

JC: I thought I saw your plums on display in the village square. . .

NIGEL: Would you like to taste my Golden Delicious?

Albert, now middle-aged, is of an age when he sleeps contentedly most of the time. He has taken over Valerie's basket in our bedroom but has a long-standing obsession with the squirrel that lives in the garden. He gets up before it gets light and takes up his sentry position by the back door, staring, quivering with anticipation. The squirrel knows he is there and taunts him through the glass. By the time Rolf gets up to let him out he is beside himself, whinnying with the pent-up desire to chase. Of course the squirrel hops out of reach and Albert is left salivating on the ground. This has been going on for years. The hopelessness of the situation never dawns on Albert. You think he'd call it a day and give up, but his endearing eternal optimism never falters. He opens his eyes at the crack of dawn each morning thinking, 'Yes! Today is the day!' Eventually, after the ritual of sneering at his pursuer for an hour or so, the squirrel moves on to next door's garden and Albert comes inside. When I've had my tea I get up and take him to the park, where there is more squirrel torture. I wondered recently if, in his mind, there is only one squirrel in the world, popping up all over the place to bait him.

Then he sleeps. If I'm doing panto, I go off for my matinee. A dog walker comes in the afternoon, Albert sleeps some more, then Rolf, who still does something or other in an office (I don't like to pry), comes home. Albert sleeps some more. Deep, satisfying rest. There are times when he just lies there, eyes open, swallowing contentedly, sighing, his limbs relaxed and floppy. Thinking. 'Tomorrow is the day I catch the squirrel. I'll be faster. I'll get up earlier. Tomorrow.' Then his eyes slowly close, he stretches and drifts off to sleep once more. Sometimes I lie with him on the sofa, spooning him and synchronising our breathing. Contentment spreads over me like warm sunshine and I doze.

You meet a good class of fellow dog walker in Regent's Park, where I have been walking one dog or another for the past twenty-five years. For the first twenty years I must have carried myself in a way that discouraged conversation – I never spoke to a soul – but these days something has changed. I find I'm very chatty. It's surprising how many people ask if the dog with me is Fanny the Wonder Dog. If it were, she'd be forty years old!

This happens so often that I realise people must recognise me and make the association without pausing to work out the chances. I get a thrill from it every time. Fanny lives on.

After spending so long in Kent, where we rarely met anyone else on walks apart from the Most Boring Man in the World, Albert has got out of the habit of socialising and, without Valerie there to pave the way, approaches any dog with suspicion. Encounters could end in a scrap and I think it wise to keep him on the lead mostly. Back in Regent's Park he retrieves his manners. He has got his confidence back.

One lady in her eighties walks two Bichon Frise, one of whom has a high sex drive, apparently. 'He has a wank blanket at home,' she informed me breezily last week.

There is a very disturbed man who walks a bewildered-looking Pomeranian (a breed that always looks to me as if it has had a lit firework shoved up its arse). The man shouts at invisible foes and makes violent threats, thrashing at the air with his fists: 'Come on, you cunts! I'll shoot the lot of ya! You killed my wife and now I'll take you out! I've got a gun!' His poor dog wanders about, pretending he's not with him, and probably he won't be for long. His owner's rants are getting more and more alarming and I fear he will be sectioned one day. Maybe his wife hasn't been killed after all, and she will care for the dog. Maybe the man will be given the correct medication and will be well again. Or maybe the dog will end up at Battersea. Albert is always nice to the wide-eyed Pomeranian – commiserating, one dog to another, about his unbalanced keeper, I suspect.

I like bumping into the arty woman I meet most mornings with her frantic border collie. She wears a fur hat in all weathers, and likes to pass comment on how awful the Tories are, how articulate the Labour leader is, or ask if I'm enjoying *The Crown*.

A huge cow-like dog called Thelma staggers around with her owner, who gives me updates on Thelma's heart condition. A recent scan revealed a plastic bottle top lodged in Thelma's throat. Thelma's breathing is much improved now it has been removed. As it would be.

No wonder, what with the squirrels and all the doggy socialising, that Albert slept so soundly during the panto run.

I managed to achieve a fifty-one-date tour called *Born to Mince* in the spring of 2019 without disturbing Albert's routine much. Due to his age and without Valerie to keep him company I didn't think he'd enjoy the dressing-room routine – besides which, theatres are a bit dog-phobic these days. Health and safety, written permissions, muzzles. Too much hassle. I walked him in the mornings if I was in residence, and our trusty dog walker did the afternoon exercise before Rolf got home. For a few weeks Rolf's father came down from Oop North. Every time Albert looked at Rolf's father, he assumed the dog wanted to go for a walk. 'Come on, then!' he'd say. Albert became very fit while I was away.

The show was the usual mix of nonsense and audience participation, which this time came in the form of Heterosexual Aversion Therapy. To show consistency, if nothing else, Joan Collins got a mention when I was talking about my glowing complexion: 'Dame Joan Collins sent me a sample pack from her Eternal Beauty range, which has a revolutionary scouring powder base. Comes with its own palette knife.'

I also described my ever-evolving health regime: 'And, of course, I don't drink any more. Well, I do, but only my own urine. Or if I can't manage it, I use the dog's. You'll find it on sale during the interval. You weren't expecting an ice cream, were you? No, I'm sorry. Kale salad with a Staffordshire bull terrier dressing. £4.50. You'll thank me for it.'

The lovely Gary Wilmot, who did panto with me each year, wrote a song for me to finish Act 1 with. In *Snow White* he played the part of Nora Crumble and we used to chat in the wings, him in full drag, me dressed as a garden rockery.

'It's a bit rude,' he cautioned.

'That won't be a problem,' I assured him.

The song for my tour was inspired by a conversation Gary overheard on the train from Milton Keynes to London. It was called 'Life's a Cunt'.

> *Even in a perfect life,*
> *A little rain must fall,*
> *But these simple words of wisdom*
> *Will help you through it all.*

When you've asked for a nice sharp steak-knife
And the knife they bring you is blunt,
Don't get in a tizz,
That's just how it is,
Sometimes
Life's a cunt.[15]

While on the road, I turned sixty. I felt a warm glow when I walked on stage at the beautiful Theatre Royal, Bury St Edmunds, and the audience sang 'Happy birthday'. Goodness, I thought. What a sobering landmark. Old age is creeping up on me like a Catholic priest in a public lavatory.

The tour finished on 6 June 2019 at the London Palladium, where I felt very much at home. It was packed to the rafters, the Palladium crew made it all look and sound wonderful, and with my friends and family there it was a riotous, joyful end to the tour. Nick was at the party afterwards, a flesh-coloured plaster covering the latest tumour blossoming on the side of his neck.

A few days later, Rolf and I went to the South of France for a week of sunshine and poker with Dame Joan. While we were away we had a new electric toilet installed. It is the Harvey Weinstein of bathroom appliances. It lights up like the Taj Mahal, has a heated seat, plays music and, best of all, has a number of prongs that will not only wash your chosen orifice but will also dry it, moisturise it and (if you're lucky enough to have one) massage your prostate and tell you a goodnight story. We became intimate very quickly.

*

Neither my husband nor I can cook. We make do. A week after our return from France we were about to sit down to a sad-looking piece of hake and an M&S salad with a bottle of chilled sauvignon blanc – to take the taste away – when my phone rang. Unknown number. It was a policeman called Geoffrey, who asked if I knew a Nick Reader. Nick had texted a neighbour asking him to call an ambulance, but by the time the emergency services arrived at his flat he was dead. A heart attack. Please could I come and identify the body? We left the food on the table, untouched, and drove to Muswell Hill in silence. Nick lay in the hallway, his head turned imperiously to one side, like the death scene of a heroine in one of his beloved operas.

Nick was one of my best friends: a remarkable man armed with a sharp and capacious intellect, an amazing, ever-expanding knowledge and understanding of all things cultural, and a dazzling wit that could never be defused, whatever life threw at him. We were brothers in arms.

I will remember Nick in many ways and in so many moments. He once sent me a quote from a *Vanity Fair* article by Jan Morris: 'I have sometimes felt, generally in moments of unexplained euphoria, that my own life has been arranged for some transcendental but unfortunately unspecified purpose: that I am supposed indeed to bear some message, or illustrate some cosmic point or other.'

I suspect the purpose – the point – was love. It usually is, after all. I shall look out for Nick when the clouds part before I go on stage in future.

*

I had planned more tour dates for the following spring, and another trip to France. We didn't know it then, of course, but 2020 was going to be a very different year and none of this would come to pass.

Thoughts of another dog were on our minds. Rolf was always looking at rescue dogs online, but nothing ever came of it. We'd ooh and ahh over a profile for an evening then forget about it the next day. I didn't see how we could feel the psychic pull towards a particular dog via the internet. What could you really tell from a photo, after all?

I had a gap between the end of the tour and the next Palladium panto. I had another Bolds book to write, but that was all. I began to feel the determined twinges with which I was only too familiar. I said to my husband that if we were to get a new dog, now was a good time and maybe we should begin looking a little more seriously. But nothing caught our eye. The weeks rolled by and our thoughts of getting another dog faded. Until one afternoon Rolf sent me a text: 'I've found a dog.'

PART FOUR
Gigi

'Every dog must have his day.'

Jonathan Swift

CHAPTER 24

Urges from Serbia

One day, maybe soon, I'd like to visit Serbia. More specifically, I'd go to a town called Niš where I will visit the graveyard. The flower ladies work there, selling blooms for locals to place on the graves of loved ones. I will show the flower ladies a few photos of a small brown, black and white mongrel no bigger than a cat and see if any of them recognise her.

There will be one – I imagine her with a weather-beaten face and kind eyes, wearing a headscarf, although I sense I may be stereotyping here. Perhaps her eyes will light up and fill with tears and she will gabble words in Serbian that I don't under-stand. I will point to the dog in the photo, then to my heart, and say, 'Gigi! My dog!' I will make the woman understand that Gigi lives with me now in London and she is very happy. But mainly I will thank the flower lady. Perhaps I'll offer her a bag of beetroot – isn't that what Serbians enjoy for a nutritious snack? I will thank her for feeding Gigi when she was living wild and feral among the tombstones.

The flower lady will be amazed that Gigi is still alive. Last time she saw her, she had been hit by a car and lay by the side of the road, apparently lifeless.

Gigi is tough. A survivor.

Tuesday 20 August 2019

I got a text from Rolf.

'I've found a dog.'

'Er, a girl?'

'Yup, Gigi. Rescue. From Serbia.'

And then he sent me her profile. Turns out he had already reserved her. . .

Jovana, from the charity Serbia's Forgotten Paws, sent us more photos, and Rolf and I had some discussion:

'Those nipples!'

'Shush . . . They're just like yours.'

'They've been well chewed on.'

'As I said, just like yours!'

'I quite like the dog on the left . . .'.

Our commitment was immediate. Does this happen on Tinder too? I wouldn't know. We didn't know much about the situation for stray dogs in Serbia, so we investigated. Animal welfare in Serbia – indeed, throughout the Balkans – has a very poor reputation. There are no exact figures but official estimates say there could be around 50,000 stray dogs. We read about Mila, a young female mutt from a Belgrade suburb. Her legs had been cut off with a power saw. She managed to recover and find a home with a new family but no one was punished, despite police pledges to find the attackers.

So, dogs in Serbia have a tough time. There are only a few dog shelters and there are thousands of abandoned animals living on the streets. Government-run dog shelters are unsavoury places, rife with cruelty and terrible methods of euthanasia. Serbia's Forgotten Paws, which rescued Gigi, is a UK-registered charity based in Niš. As well as rescuing dogs and finding homes for them in the UK, it runs a catch, neuter and release scheme in the local area to humanely control the population of stray cats and dogs. It is run by ten unpaid volunteers.

So this was where our new dog was coming from. All this heart-breaking information only made us more determined to bring Gigi into our home. She would be one of the lucky ones. We filled out the paperwork and waited patiently for information. Finally we were told that she was on her way – travelling in a lorry with fourteen other dogs from Serbia through Austria, Germany and France. She would cross the Channel by ferry then have to spend two days in quarantine at Dover before the last leg of her journey, to a centre in Surrey from where we would be able to collect her.

On a sunny Saturday in September, with Albert sitting in the back seat, we drove nervously down a mud track in Cobham and followed signs to a local doggy Day Care Centre.

'What if we don't like her?' I asked.

'We will,' said Rolf. 'But if we don't get on, there is a three-week fostering period before we have to fully commit.'

Jovana from Serbia's Forgotten Paws was waiting by the gate to greet us, and we could hear excited barking nearby. My heart was in my mouth and I already felt tearful. We went through to a large field where a pack of dogs of all shapes and sizes ran around excitedly, free at last after being cooped up in cages for the journey then confined in quarantine. We let Albert off his lead and he ploughed in to meet the Serbian dogs. A couple of other people were wandering about, also there to collect dogs.

I was surprised how healthy and happy they all looked – I had expected former street dogs to be thin and flea-bitten. Jovana explained that they had all been fostered for several months, health-checked, groomed, fed and assessed before they were put up for adoption. All the dogs were in good condition and all looked handsome and happy. There were two blonde, shaggy dogs that were probably related and were going to be rehomed together. There was a boisterous boxer and a chunky, slow Burmese type of dog.

'He is old,' said Jovana, giving his back a rub. 'When they don't have long, we like to home them so their last few years, at least, will be happy ones. We don't like them to end their days in the shelter. There are some kind people who always take the older dogs.'

'Where is Gigi?' I asked, unable to contain myself any longer.

'Er . . .' said Jovana, scanning the field. 'She will be up to no good somewhere, I expect.'

'Oh my God, there she is!' declared Rolf. A flash of tan sped past us in pursuit of a bigger dog. She was tiny. And fast.

'Gigi!' I called. She stopped running and turned to look. I got a treat out and bent down, hand outstretched. She came tentatively towards me, her ears pricked, her eyes fixed on the treat, occasionally flicking up to look at me. She took the treat and chewed it quite slowly, as if it was a new taste she wasn't quite sure if she liked. Then she stayed, looking me up and down. Curious. Amused.

'She looks very like Fanny,' I said softly to Rolf. 'The eyes – exactly the same!'

She also had the same basic tan colouring with a darker back and snout, and white chest and paws. Eyes the colour of Bristol cream sherry. She was a very neat, well-proportioned dog, although not over-endowed when it came to leg length, with a small, suspiciously stumpy tail. I crouched down to stroke her head. Her eyes softened.

'You're Gigi, are you?' I asked gently. 'Shall I pick you up?'

I slipped my hand under her ribcage, lifted her up slowly and held her to my chest. She was no heavier than a chicken from the supermarket. I expected her to stiffen or pull away, perhaps be a little wary of me, but the opposite happened. She leant into me and sighed, rested her head on my neck and stayed very still, as if this was the moment she had been waiting for. Or so I imagined.

'There, then. What do you think of that?' I asked Gigi, slipping another treat into her mouth.

'She's got a lot of teeth,' said Rolf.

'You hold her while I have a look,' I said, passing Gigi over. Yes, she had a lot of nice white small teeth and four rather over-large canines, the top two overlapping her bottom lip. Her nipples were quite pronounced.

'Has she had puppies?' I asked Jovana.

She shrugged. 'Possibly.'

'And what happened to her tail?'

This was also a mystery. An accident. Maybe someone cut it off. . .

Jovana told us what she knew of Gigi's story. She had been dumped by the cemetery in Niš. In Serbia there are many flower shops. The flower ladies fed her, as they did all the stray dogs in the area – the charity, which is nearby, donates the food. One of the flower ladies saw Gigi get knocked by a car and was certain she'd be dead because she was so tiny. She called the charity and one of the workers came to collect Gigi. They got her to the shelter and called the vet. Amazingly, she survived. They watched over her for a few days and that was it: rather than release her back to the cemetery, they decided to put her up on the Serbia's Forgotten Paws website, where Rolf spotted her.

We filled out the necessary paperwork and introduced Gigi to Albert, who seemed delighted with her and her gentle, slightly comical nature. Then we drove home. Gigi sat on my lap, shaking, the whole way – fearful, no doubt, that she was embarking on another long journey into the unknown. I did my best to comfort her, but we were all relieved when we got back home to Camden and into the garden. She looked worried, and stayed by Albert's side. He seemed exhausted by the day's events and the realisation that Gigi was here to stay.

*

The first night, she slept quietly in the lounge. Maybe she knew she was home at last and could relax. 'How good she is!' we declared.

Little did we know. . .

CHAPTER 25

The Beast from the East Emerges

For a couple of days, Gigi bided her time. She presented herself as a sweet, simpering girl. She was shy and gentle, content to lie quietly in her basket waggling her stump or trot around the park on her extendable lead, shy with strangers, Bambi-like with other dogs. This all changed on the third evening. We were relaxing on the sofa with Albert between us when Gigi walked into the room. She contemplated us for a moment before launching herself through the air in our direction, like a flying monkey. She landed on a startled Albert and rolled onto her back, a glint in her eye, her legs splayed, mouth open, displaying her fangs. Albert sat up, looking worried, and after a few satisfied grunting noises, like a pensioner finishing a Sudoku, she closed her jaws around his ankle and shook her head, twisting his leg painfully in the process.

'What's happened to her?' asked Rolf, alarmed. Albert was clearly wondering the same thing as he jumped off the sofa and limped out of the way.

'She's playing, I think,' I said, placing my hand on Gigi's

tummy and giving her a scratch. Still on her back, she squirmed from side to side, huffed and puffed then began kicking her back legs in circles, like an upturned clockwork toy.

'She's a bit manic,' observed Rolf.

'Maybe she feels that she can be herself now. She's more confident,' I offered uncertainly.

'She's like a completely different dog, though.'

This was indeed the case. As we spoke, Gigi flipped herself onto her feet and with a throaty growl of (we hoped) mock aggression, she leapt onto my chest and stared into my eyes for a second before hopping like a baby kangaroo onto Rolf, then onto the floor in search of Albert. With a look of determined mischief, she barged into him then dived for his back legs, clamping her jaws around his ankle again. Bewildered, he reached down to her with his mouth. In what looked like a planned manoeuvre, she swiftly moved her grip to his exposed throat. He keeled over, and she was on top of him in a second, clinging to his lip. When he shook her off, she went for his ears then his jowls, nipping and growling. Albert had no choice but to join in the game of (very) rough and (lots of) tumble. He hadn't done that sort of adolescent wrestling for years, and there was a slight air of embarrassment about him as he played. But Gigi was like a ferret on speed, and it was hard to maintain dignity in the situation. As far as she was concerned, ears, eyes and genitals were all fair game.

When things reached a frenzy, we thought we should put a stop to it and separate them. I lifted a panting Gigi off poor Albert, who did his best to regain his dignity by going to the kitchen for a very long drink of water.

So. Gigi had shown her true colours – a Jekyll-and-Hyde hound. Delightful and charming one minute, murderous psycho the next. She could turn on a sixpence, and it became apparent over the following weeks that it wasn't just Albert who was a target. She could be asleep on my lap like a baby antelope and her eyes would slowly open. In a flash I was dealing with Villanelle in a homicide scene from *Killing Eve*. We'd go from *Toy Story* to slasher film in a nanosecond.

The saving grace in all this was her size. Her teeth were sharp, but she didn't have the jaw power to do any serious damage. She wasn't really mad, we decided. She was acting crazy. Maybe it was a Serbian thing? Their idea of fun, perhaps. Are they big on vampires there? Blood and biting could be part of their culture. And we had to make allowances for her past. Only a few weeks ago she was living rough, knee-deep in Balkan mud and faeces. Being so tiny, she must have had to fight to survive. Developing a 'Don't mess with me or I'll chew off your cock, you cunt,' attitude with the wild dogs of the Niš graveyard was a survival technique to save her from being brushed aside or possibly devoured as a light snack. If there was one dead pigeon to feed ten hungry strays, then only a killer attitude and a spot of canine karate would get her to the front of the queue, otherwise she'd have gone hungry or starved.

It was going to take her a while to acclimatise to her new, sophisticated world here in London town, I thought. Her uncouth ways, the biting and the sudden mood changes would fade away with time. . . But no. Gigi hasn't changed. We wouldn't want her to, in fact. We've grown to love her unpredictable nature. It's like living with Bette Davis on crack.

'Is she in a mood?' we ask. 'Watch out, Albert. She's got that look in her eye. . .'.

Albert is very accepting of Gigi's funny ways, but he does need to escape sometimes. We have a stairgate so we can separate them when she is in full Aileen Wuornos mode. Gigi also, for reasons known only to herself, refuses to come up the stairs to the bedroom, preferring to sleep on her faux fur bed in the lounge, so a night-time respite for us all is more or less guaranteed.

Of course, there are times when her softer side emerges. The afternoon 'sit-down' is an essential part of her routine and we (or whoever has charge of her) are required to comply between 2.15 p.m. and 3 p.m. Then she is quiet and soft and adorable.

She is a many-layered dog, like an onion. Her initial sweetness masked a feistiness which, it took me a while to realise, was in fact fear – much like yobs who shout insults at gays are afraid – in their case, of their own suppressed desires. On the way to the park, Gigi took to barking at white cars or vans. The best way to stop this was to pick her up, and it was only when I held her close that I could feel her thumping heart and trembling limbs. She was fearful of these vehicles and trying to shoo them away. Maybe it was a white car that knocked her over back in Niš and she has traumatic associations? Perfectly understandable, if so. I'm the same with maroon cars (school uniform; miserable time) although I don't bark. I just refuse to get in them.

But whatever the reason for her frequent vocal displays, we have to face the fact that Gigi is quite a yappy dog. And her yaps are rather shrill. She puts me in mind of a musical theatre type practising for an audition.

Another curiosity that has come to light is where and when Gigi relieves herself. For some reason, she has decided that the garden is not a suitable place. No, she must go 'out'. She won't even consider squatting on the decking or the flower beds. Consequently, early each morning and late every night either Rolf or I have to put on our coat and shoes and shuffle around the block with her, much as I did with Fanny all those years ago. Who knows why this is, but we have got used to it.

A danger we have learned about the hard way is Gigi's tendency to bolt when scared. Sudden loud noises – which are difficult to foresee – cause her to take flight. It has happened twice, and both occasions were terrifying. In a manoeuvre so quick we still don't know how she did it, she freed herself from her harness and ran for her life.

Rolf took Gigi and Albert to his mysterious office in Shoreditch one day, and the clanking of a metal shutter being raised panicked her. She was off, shooting down the pavement, leaving Rolf holding her lead and empty harness. He thrust Albert's lead and his briefcase into the hands of a complete stranger. 'Hold these for me!' he commanded and sprinted after the crazed Gigi. He managed to grab her, but she leapt from his grasp and sped off again. With an athletic prowess he didn't know he had, he managed to catch up with her again and grabbed her – within yards of four lanes of thundering traffic. She was petrified and so was he. He still has flashbacks.

A few weeks later I was walking her down Camden High Street. A police siren suddenly started up right next to us. I felt the lead jerk. I looked down and the harness was empty. Gigi was running ahead, weaving between shoppers. My dignity as a local celebrity forgotten, I shrieked her name and gave chase. 'Stop her!' But she was too fast and slippery for anyone to succeed. My pursuit was just making her run even faster, I realised. I had to try something else. Remembering I had a dog treat in my pocket, I stopped and called, 'Gigi! What's this?' in a cheerful, sing-song voice – under the circumstances, a remarkable bit of acting. It worked. She stopped and turned back to me. Anything for a grain-free 80 per cent fish treat, clearly. I gave her the treat and picked her up, our hearts thumping like a pair of coked-up disco dollies.

When I took her to the park the next day, wearing a freshly purchased, extra-snug and secure harness, word of my drama outside the Pound Shop had reached the other dog walkers. 'I hear you were practising rugby tackles on the high street yesterday,' chortled one.

I am constantly aware that any loud noise – siren, horn or engine – will spook Gigi and I have to pick her up at once. Sometimes just the look of a vehicle will upset her, and she will look up at me and I'll lift her to safety.

But it isn't funny. It is the stuff of nightmares. To lose a dog to natural causes is bad enough – God forbid, seeing my dog being run over would be too much to bear. It happened to Fanny once and she miraculously survived. Not again. I'd need sedation and counselling.

Gigi has no time for cyclists, either. Possibly due to another trauma, or it could be common sense. They are very shouty and aggressive, cycling around Regent's Park in sinister packs, especially when they have to suffer annoying pedestrians and dog walkers on zebra crossings. A taxi driver told me recently that 'the ones wearing Lycra are all on steroids, you know,' and I've no reason to suppose he was lying.

'How's Fanny the Wonder Dog?' asked the same taxi driver.

'She died twenty-one years ago,' I replied.

'I had a dog called Nookie once,' he went on, as they do. 'Got him for my wife after she had a miscarriage. This was back in the sixties. I was living in the East End. I had to go out at night shouting "Nookie! Nookie!"'

I laughed politely. I'd been expecting this punchline.

Another tell-tale sign of Gigi's origin is her taste for muck and filth. When out and about she veers away from grassy knolls or cheery flower beds. Instead she is drawn to piles of rubbish and rotting food. She likes nothing more than a spot of human excrement or a used syringe. To be honest, I don't really need to go to Niš. I can imagine what it is like.

But we have grown to know and love Gigi and her funny ways – and she ours. She loves me, Rolf and Albert, but mainly me. I have never known such passionate adoration – and I once went out with a sales assistant from Dobbies. She lies on my chest and gazes at me in wonderment at every opportunity. I swear her eyeballs throb with love for me. True, she might conclude the love-in with nipping my chin or chewing on my finger, but it's only because she cares.

What Albert thinks of Gigi is another question. I do detect a certain worried look in his eyes when she approaches him, and he definitely assumes the brace position if she is in one of her inverted hara-kiri moods. This usually happens on the playing fields, when she is overcome with a murderous combination of excitement and pent-up energy. She will charge at him from a distance and when she reaches him she becomes a whirling dervish of teeth and fur. She bites and tears, grabbing him anywhere she can, shaking her mouthful of tender flesh from side to side. Albert whimpers his distress and has learned to curl up in a ball to protect his extremities. Luckily, I know the signs now and make sure I'm on hand to stop her before she draws blood. I scoop her off him, a wriggling devil dog, teeth gnashing the air like a cartoon hyena, and she stops at once. My human touch and firm voice cast out the demon like an exorcism, and she becomes calm. Her eyes lose their red glow and peace is restored. The whole business only lasts a few seconds. Poor Albert. We are considering a muzzle. For her, not him.

Goldilocks and the Three Bears was the 2019/20 panto offering at the Palladium, and I was cast as the Ringmaster. The jokes wrote themselves: 'My Dick won an Olivier, but there's no knowing what my ring will pick up this year.'

Paul O'Grady was back in the building as my rival, the evil Baron von Savage, and we more or less picked up where we'd left off in *Cinderella*. Panto at the Palladium wouldn't be the same if I didn't receive a letter from Medway. This one was along the same lines as the previous one: it was written in a Christmas card but with 'Merry Christmas' sternly crossed out. Pleasingly, it was a little angrier this time:

CLARY

ONCE AGAIN YOU HAVE UPSET FAMILYS [SIC]
WATCHING THE PANTO. YOUR FOUL-MOUTHED
INNUENDO'S [SIC] FORCED MOTHERS TO WALK
OUT WITH THEIR CHILDREN IN DISGUST AT YOUR
FILTHY COMMENTS.

YOU AND YOUR KIND SHOULD NEVER BE ALLOWED
NEAR CHILDREN. YOU NASTY PERVERT AND PAEDO
YOU SHOULD BE ON THE SEX OFFENDERS LIST.

I noted that I had been upgraded to all capital letters this time, which was thrilling, and clearly another indication that the sap was rising. Spontaneous combustion may lie ahead, I fear.

After the panto, Rolf and I decided against our usual holiday in the sun. It was clear that my father was reaching the final stages of his illness, and I wanted to spend time with him. I'm writing this in the room in which my father spent his last few weeks, and I don't think he'd thank me for talking about him here. He'd say it was none of your business. He would be right.

How was death achieved? Deftly, mid-sentence, as it transpires.

My mother plunged from sixty-seven years of marriage into a world pandemic where she must shield and isolate, go nowhere and see no one.

'It's unfortunate,' she said with heroic understatement. But every evening she sits with Meg the cat on her lap and Whiskey the dog by her side. She is not alone.

We watch and learn from our parents, whatever our age.

CHAPTER 26

A Dog is for Life – a Life is for Dogs

All my adult life I have had a dog by my side. Bearing witness, steadying me, restraining me if I'm being reckless, bringing me back to the present moment and giving me daily lessons in compassion and kindness.

Valerie and Fanny hum their presence to me still from their respective receptacles.

Albert has demonstrated saintly patience since Gigi's arrival. Placidity and tolerance are the gifts he brings: he is the yin to Gigi's yang. I remember his tenacity with Valerie when he first arrived, and it is an essential part of his character. He love-bombed her until she gave in. He's like a nightlight of positivity, an eternal glow of cheerfulness made fur.

As I walked the dogs today in Regent's Park, Albert pottered happily about and Gigi chased a pigeon as she always does, with serious intent. To catch and to eat. She has a passion for discarded corks. She will smell one a hundred yards off, buried in the grass, and run to get it, then toss it in the air and catch it. Perhaps in her graveyard days she was befriended by the local winos and corks were in plentiful supply, tossed her way when a bottle was empty.

I used to wonder how Gigi survived such harsh conditions. But that was when I knew only the sweet, simpering Gigi. Now I've seen the roaring lion within, all has become clear. Gigi could survive on Mars. She'd rip the face off a passing Martian if need be, or eat dust and drink her own urine. That's my girl. That's what she has taught me. Survival. Fighting spirit. Optimism.

I think back to her Serbian origins. Her journey seems vaguely mythical: living in a graveyard among the dead, helped by beneficent flower women. Someone better educated than I might find parallels with some Greek myth or other. A quick google tells me Iris (a native flower to Serbia) is the goddess of the rainbow which, as everyone knows, is our gay emblem. She is also the messenger of the gods. Was Gigi sent by the gods as a blessing on our gay marriage? A fanciful notion. There is always the possibility, given her temperament, that she might have been sent as a curse. I'm sure my friend from Medway would think so.

But lily of the valley, another Serbian flower, symbolises the return of happiness. Yes. Although I fantasise about finding the person who dumped Gigi in the graveyard, what would I say if I did? What would I do? Gigi has had the last laugh: a happy life.

I leave you with a typical evening scene. I have phoned my mother and all is well. She isn't lonely because she has Meg on her lap, Whiskey beside her, and a gin and tonic in her hand.

Rolf and I are on the sofa in Camden watching the evening news, and I am administering my husband's daily foot massage.

Beside me is a working script for my next tour and underneath that a copy of *The Dresser*, which is another project scheduled for the autumn. But who knows?

Albert is wedged between us, under Rolf's outstretched legs, in a deep, noisy sleep. Gigi is beside me. She lies on her back, pressed against my left thigh, her rump tucked into the crook of my arm, her head lolling off the seat, mouth slightly open, showing her generous collection of tiny teeth. She gives a contented moan and swallows twice. Her eyes close and she sleeps – just so long as I continue to gently scratch her neck. If I stop for more than three seconds, her eyes open to devil-dog slits and she turns her head and bares her teeth. She may bite one of us soon if she feels like it.

The newsreader talks of the world pandemic, of deaths and infections, and the new normal. We change channels and watch some allegedly beautiful young people living together in a villa looking for love. We make disparaging remarks as Albert snores . . . and out of the corner of my eye I see Gigi's jaws closing in on my husband's toes.

THE END